MAN OF
SORROWS

Other books by Gerald Wheeler:

Beyond Life
Saints and Sinners
Wisdom
James White

To order, call 1-800-765-6955.

Visit us at www.reviewandherald.com for information on other Review and Herald® products.

MAN OF SORROWS

GOD, SALVATION, AND
THE BOOK OF ISAIAH

GERALD WHEELER

REVIEW AND HERALD® PUBLISHING ASSOCIATION
HAGERSTOWN, MD 21740

This book was
Edited by Raymond H. Woolsey
Copyedited by James Cavil
Designed by Freshcut Design
Cover illustration by Lars Justinen/Justinen Creative Group
Typeset: Bembo 11/13

PRINTED IN U.S.A.

08 07 06 05 04   5 4 3 2 1

R&H Cataloging Service
Wheeler, Gerald William, 1943-   .
    Man of sorrows.

    1. Bible. O.T. Isaiah—Study and teaching.
I. Title.

                    224.1

ISBN 0-8280-1824-3

To Larissa

May she grow to see the power
of the Holy One of Israel

CONTENTS

INTRODUCTION

Many people, when they hear mention of the book of Isaiah, will immediately hear in their minds the haunting strains of Handel's *Messiah*: "Wonderful Counselor, the Mighty God, the Everlasting Father, the Prince of Peace." Others regard Isaiah as the book of the Bible that most often predicts the coming of Jesus as Messiah. He is the Suffering Servant born of a virgin, the Man of Sorrows. Christ Himself referred to passages in Isaiah, employing one of them to announce His mission in the synagogue at Nazareth (Luke 4:16-21). Philip used Isaiah 53:7, 8 to teach the Ethiopian eunuch "the good news about Jesus" (Acts 8:26-39). The New Testament consistently cites or alludes to the book of Isaiah.

Still others see Isaiah as a source for end-time scenarios. The book has much to say about how the Lord will set up His kingdom on earth, becoming the God of the nations. It depicts a restored earth on which peace and security will reign forever.

But Isaiah is even more than this. It is the story of the warfare between good and evil. The prophet reveals that the conflicts we witness in this world mirror a larger struggle between supernatural powers. This war rages from heaven, the center of the universe, to Judah, a tiny nation caught up in the geopolitics of the ancient Near East. Judah's struggle with Assyria and the other nations has cosmic significance. When human kings go to war and plunge the world into sorrow, their actions mirror the conflict between two invisible kingdoms. The God of the nations combats a cosmic usurper who has set up his own kingdom on earth. Yet in the book of Isaiah this conflict ends in a scenario that is surprisingly peaceful as compared to the messages of later prophets who do not take the story that far.

Throughout Isaiah the larger world—the cosmic, the supernatural—keeps wanting to burst into this one. The prophet's language strains beyond his place and time. It points to more than just his contemporary situation. At times we are not sure which he has in mind—the earthly realm or the supernatural. Every now and then in Isaiah the surface of our reality is ripped away, revealing the greater reality beyond. We constantly encounter individuals and events that at first glance might seem to be merely human and earthly, but upon closer examination we catch glimpses of something far vaster and more important.

That is why interpreters struggle over such issues as who is the king of Babylon in Isaiah 14, and is the "servant" mentioned so frequently just God's people or something more—perhaps even divine? Who is the Man of Sorrows, and what will He accomplish? As we read through the book we will meet judgments on specific nations that are described in language that is global in nature, and hear a taunt against a tyrannical human being who has flashes of the satanic shining through him. Not until the New Testament will inspiration pull aside some of the curtain of this world and more fully reveal the identity of those involved in this conflict and the nature of their warfare.

The book of Isaiah has perhaps the greatest depiction of God's role in the struggle between Him and the forces of evil in the whole Old Testament. The book of Revelation finds in Isaiah's portrayal of this both earthly and cosmic war a rich source of allusions. For example, compare Isaiah 8:7 with Revelation 17:15; Isaiah 13:21 with Revelation 18:2; the series of images in Isaiah 47 with those in Revelation 18, as well as those of Isaiah 60 and 65 with those of Revelation 21; and Isaiah 55:1 with Revelation 22:17.

Isaiah especially stresses the Lord's role as Creator and Ruler of the nations. The book sees in God's power to create His greatest proof that He is the one and only true God, the fundamental trait that distinguishes between Him and idols (Isa. 40:26, 28; 42:5; 44:24; 45:12, 18; 48:13; 51:16). As Richard Bauckham observes, Judaism believed that "only the God of Israel is worthy of worship because he is sole Creator of all things and sole Ruler of all things."[1] As the writers of the New Testament described Jesus in divine imagery borrowed from the book of Isaiah, early Christians began to realize that Christ as Creator and Ruler of all things was also fully God.[2] The study of Isaiah enabled them to grasp more completely who He really was. The book's witness to Jesus is far more than just that of the Suffering Servant and the child named Immanuel, "God with us."

Isaiah the Human Being

As is the pattern throughout the Old Testament, Scripture does not give much biographical information about Isaiah. Apart from individuals such as David, Moses, the patriarchs of Genesis, and a few others such as Elijah, Elisha, and Hezekiah, most people in the Bible appear briefly, then vanish. Isaiah is no exception.

The prophet Isaiah, son of Amoz, lived and worked in Jerusalem from at least about 750 B.C. to 700 B.C. The name Isaiah means "Yahweh [is] salvation." His book says that he served under four kings—Uzziah, Jotham, Ahaz, and Hezekiah—and that he had intimate contact with them. Because of his ready access to these kings, tradition has suggested that he belonged to the royal family and even may have been a cousin of King Uzziah. But it was also common practice in the ancient Near East for prophets to approach the king and his court and to be involved in such religious activities as Temple worship. The ancients considered prophets to be chosen by the gods, and that gave them special privileges; so Isaiah did not need to be of royal descent to have the king's attention.

As prophet, Isaiah had to deal with situations in Judah that were as complex as any we see in today's headlines. Many Bible readers assume that both Judah and Israel went into steady decline after the breakup of the united monarchy after the death of Solomon. But archaeological and other evidence indicate that the two kingdoms experienced various rises and falls, depending at least in part upon the political situation of the surrounding nations. During periods when the influence of Egypt and Assyria waned, both Judah and Israel could become quite powerful. One of these periods occurred during Isaiah's youth. King Uzziah built Judah into a strong commercial and military state. He constructed extensive fortifications throughout the land, had a large standing army, established a seaport on the Red Sea, increased trade, received tribute from the Ammonites, and successfully waged war against the Philistines and the Arabians. Judah achieved a level of prosperity and strength not seen since the days of Solomon.

But the new wealth brought its own problems. It led to economic oppression and avarice, as well as formality in religious matters. Prosperity developed a preoccupation with materialism. Because people in Old Testament times equated such prosperity with divine approval, many in Judah would have assumed that God was definitely on their side and thus condoned their actions.

Uzziah reigned for 52 years. But about the time that his son Jotham assumed sole rule, Assyria began to revive as the dominant power in the region. Tiglath-pileser (reigned 745-727 B.C.) sent his forces westward and conquered a number of territories near Judah. As we shall see later, an attempt to resist Assyria's expansion involved Jotham's son, Ahaz, in what many call the Syro-Ephraimitic war (734 B.C.). By the time Hezekiah ascended the throne, Judah was in decline and faced increasing danger from Assyria. The greatest threat came when Sennacherib attacked Jerusalem itself. We will explore these events in more detail later.

Isaiah 8:3 indicates that Isaiah was married to a woman who also had a prophetic calling. He had two sons, both of whom received symbolic names (Isa. 7:1-17; 8:1-4). In Isaiah 20 God commissioned the prophet to walk about Jerusalem wearing only a loincloth instead of his usual prophetic costume of sackcloth and sandals, to protest the Jerusalem leadership's pro-Egyptian policies. In addition, he prophesied Jerusalem's deliverance from Sennacherib (Isa. 36; 37; cf. 2 Kings 18:13-19:37), told Hezekiah of his terminal illness and eventual healing (Isa. 38; cf. 2 Kings 20:1-11), and notified him of the Lord's displeasure at Hezekiah's involvement with the envoys of the rebellious vassal king, Merodach-baladan (Isa. 39; cf. 2 Kings 20:12-19).

After chapter 39 Isaiah no longer refers to himself—his book focuses on both the future threat from Babylon and God's promises to establish a kingdom of peace and prosperity. The Lord would establish a kingdom that would eventually encompass all the nations of the earth.

Only tradition tells us anything about Isaiah's life after Hezekiah's time. At least as early as the second century A.D. the belief circulated that King Manasseh, Hezekiah's son, had martyred the prophet because of some speeches that Isaiah had made about God and Jerusalem that the king regarded as against the law. The apocryphal Ascension of Isaiah and the Mishnah have him perishing under Manasseh, and some see the reference in Hebrews 11:37 to heroes of faith being "sawed in two" as describing the prophet's fate.

The Book of Isaiah

Because of stylistic and other factors, most modern scholars regard the book of Isaiah as composed of two or more separate documents. Such scholars conclude that chapters 1-39 were by one author (often called First Isaiah or Isaiah of Jerusalem) and the remaining chapters by a second and even third writer, the latter composing their works many centuries later. Finally, an editor (referred to by scholars by the term "redactor") wove the various strands together.

But this concept is still only a scholarly conjecture. We have no physical proof that any part of the book ever existed as a separate document.

Isaiah was one of the favorite books of those who collected the Dead Sea scrolls. Archaeologists have found 21 whole or partial manuscripts in the caves around Qumran, including one leather scroll (1QIsaᵃ) copied about 125 B.C. Only the Psalms (37 manuscripts) and Deuteronomy (30 manuscripts) appeared more frequently. The version used in the scrolls is basically identical to the Masoretic text we know today.[3] Interestingly, the Dead Sea scroll versions of Isaiah have chapter 40 following 39 without any break. The only indication of any break, strangely enough, appears between chapters 33 and 34.[4]

Even those who believe that Isaiah consists of originally separate strands also recognize that the book is not haphazardly arranged but carefully structured. W. H. Brownlee, after attempting to study the composition of the book from the perspective of an ancient Near Eastern author rather than a modern Western one, pointed out that such ancient authors frequently organized their books in two parts, perhaps because of the difficulty of copying them on bulky scrolls. Thus Isaiah might have been composed in two volumes of 33 chapters each. But even then the two volumes were carefully balanced, paralleling each other, as we see from the chart below.

Subject	First half	Second half
Ruin and restoration	1-5	34, 35
Biographical material	6-8	36-40
Agents of divine blessing and judgment	9-12	41-45
Oracles against foreign powers	13-23	46-48
Universal redemption and the deliverance of Israel	24-27	49-55
Ethical sermons	28-31	56-59
Restoration of the nation	32, 33	60-66[5]

Besides general themes, detailed wordings also tie the sections of the book together. The book is a carefully constructed whole. For example, the title the "Holy One of Israel" appears 12 times in chapters 1-39 and 14 times in chapters 40-66, but elsewhere in the Old Testament only six times. At least 25 Hebrew words appear in both halves but do not occur in any other prophetic book. Such images as Isaiah's use of fire as a symbol of punishment (Isa. 1:31; 10:17; 26:11; 33:11-14; 34:9, 10; 66:24), the designation of God as "the Mighty One of Jacob/Israel" (Isa. 1:24; 49:26; 60:16), references to the "holy mountain" of Jerusalem (Isa. 2:2-4; 11:9; 27:13; 56:7; 57:13; 65:25; 66:20), and the highway to Jerusalem (Isa. 11:16; 40:3, 4; 57:14; 62:10) weave the book together.[6] Both halves of Isaiah describe Israel as "blind" (Isa. 29:18; 35:5; 42:16-18), "deaf" (Isa. 29:18; 35:5; 42:8; 43:8), forsaken of the Lord (Isa. 1:28; 65:11), "ransomed of the Lord" (Isa. 35:10; 51:11), and "the work of my hands" (Isa. 29:23; 60:21).

Derek Kidner shows how the first half of the book anticipates themes developed in the second half. "God's sovereignty in history (a major theme of 40-66) is expressed by Sennacherib in 37:26 (701 BC) in the very tone and terms of the later chapters: 'Have you not heard?' (*cf.* 46:11); 'now I have brought it to pass' (*cf.* 48:3). There is similar language on this theme in 22:11. On the 'greater exodus', ch. 35 not only matches the finest eloquence of chs. 40-66 . . . but also, in almost every verse, uses the special idioms of 1-39. Again, in the visions of ultimate concord, the passages 11:6-9 and 65:25 can scarcely be told apart."[7]

As a result of such study, even many scholars who believe that Isaiah consists of separate sources have concluded that the book must be approached as a carefully prepared whole. For example, Brevard S. Childs, although he accepts the idea that the book originated from a number of independent strands, states that to concentrate on them "fails to reckon with the book's canonical authority as a coherent witness in its final received form to the ways of God with Israel."[8]

The only book of Isaiah we have to study is the present version (no matter how it may have come to be written), and we will approach it that way in this volume.

The Theology of Isaiah

At first glance the book of Isaiah may still seem a patchwork of unrelated material. But throughout, it focuses on "the Holy One of Israel" (Isa.1:4; 5:19), who must punish His rebellious people (1:2). The book depicts Israel as a trampled vineyard (5:1-7). Having abandoned justice and righteousness (5:7; 10:1, 2), they are spiritually blind and deaf (6:9, 10; 42:7). Scripture refers to the divine judgment God will bring upon them as "the day of the Lord." But they will not be its only recipient. While Israel has already experienced a taste of its terror (5:30; 42:25), other nations will encounter its full intensity (2:11, 17, 20).

Although God must punish His people, its purpose is to redeem them (41:14, 16). He will have compassion on them (14:1, 2), leading them in a New Exodus (43:2, 16-19; 52:10-12). In His divine love God redeems

(35:9; 41:14) and saves them (43:3; 49:8). The nations bring Israel home as the Messianic age of peace and safety begins (11:6-9). A king descended from David will rule it (9:7; 32:1). God calls Him "my servant" in Isaiah 42-53, and the righteous king's suffering leads to salvation. Not only does the Servant redeem Israel, but He becomes a "light to the Gentiles" (42:6, KJV), so that those nations that had previously faced judgment (13-23) now also find salvation (55:4, 5). Wicked kings will no longer oppress God's people (11:14; 45:14). Instead, the inhabitants of all nations will flock to Jerusalem (2:2-4). Both Israel (41:8, 9; 42:1) and the Gentiles (54:17) become servants in the image of the Messianic Servant. And Jerusalem will truly be the "City of the Lord" (60:14).

Literary Characteristics

From a literary perspective Isaiah is perhaps the most sophisticated book of the Old Testament. It has the largest vocabulary. While Ezekiel uses 1,535 different words, Jeremiah 1,653, and the psalmists 2,170, Isaiah employs 2,186. The book consists of both prose (mostly in Isaiah 36-39) and poetry. The styles of poetry include oracles (for example, Isa. 13-23), a wisdom poem (28:23-29; cf. 32:5-8), hymns of praise (12; 38:10-20), a national lament (63:7-64:12), and apocalyptic-like material (24-27).

The biblical author displayed his skill and creativity by the wide spectrum of literary techniques he employed. Isaiah especially enjoyed personification. The prophet depicts the sun and moon as ashamed (24:23), the desert rejoicing (35:1), mountains and forests bursting into song (44:23), and trees clapping hands (55:12). He liked epigrams and metaphors, the latter especially involving flood, storms, and sound (1:13; 5:18, 22; 8:8; 10:22; 28:17, 20; 30:28, 30).

Other literary devices he used include antithesis (contrasting opposites) and alliteration (1:18; 3:24; 17:10, 12), hyperbole and parable (2:7; 5:1-7; 28:23-29), word play (5:7; 7:9), and rhetorical questions and dialogue (6:8; 10:8-11). The taunting poems of Isaiah 14:4-23 and Isaiah 37:22-29 and the sarcasm of Isaiah 44:9-20 illustrate additional literary techniques. The prophet's literary skill shows through even in translation, making his book one of the most beautiful in the Bible. The book presents great themes in the form of great literature.

What Is a Prophet?

Isaiah was a prophet. When most people hear the word "prophet," they think of someone predicting the future. But that is only a small part of the prophetic role. The prophet's primary work is that of being the conscience of God's people. The Lord of the universe sends prophets to guide His people when they get off course, and to summon them back when they have wandered away.

If you study the messages of the prophets, including that of Isaiah, you will discover that they really speak relatively little about the future except for the consequences of rebellion and apostasy or what God would like to do for His people if only they would return their allegiance to Him. Instead, they call for their listeners and readers, whether king or common people, to do righteously, to care for others, to deal with others in love and justice. Prophets may spend more time protesting the dishonest business practices of the wealthy than they do announcing the future arrival of the Messiah or the destruction of the world.

Speaking to All Nations

Because of space limitations, we will not be able to examine every passage or explore every theme. Some sections we will have to pass over. But one theme we will touch upon in passing is that Isaiah could reach not only to his own people but to the surrounding Gentiles as well. God spoke through the prophet in ways that other nations could understand. He employed widespread concepts and images of Isaiah's time, not just esoteric symbols or language restricted to His own people. Some of them even came from non-Israelite culture. If the Lord of Israel and Judah was to become the God of the nations, the rest of the world would have to understand His plans for them.

As these shared concepts struck a response in the hearts of the nations, they too would long for many of the things that God promised His people: a peaceable, righteous kingdom; the end of suffering and sickness; and a world restored. When Scripture uses a concept or image, however, it does not mean that it endorses it in every detail. Many times the Lord would correct or even combat a certain concept. But such illusions provide a beginning point that allows Him or the prophet to communicate a bit of greater truth.

And we continue to do that today. Even those, for example, who do not believe that people go straight to heaven when they die may still use a story about Saint Peter standing at the gates of heaven as a sermon illustration to get some other concept across to the congregation.

Too often today Christians speak and write in imagery and concepts that do not communicate to the world around us. Perhaps we could learn something from the way God spoke through His biblical prophets.

But the most important thing we can gain from Isaiah is the good news of the God of the nations and what He wants to do for all humanity, especially through the mysterious figure of the Man of Sorrows.

---

[1] Richard Bauckham, *God Crucified: Monotheism and Christology in the New Testament* (Grand Rapids: William B. Eerdmans Pub. Co., 1998), p. 11.

[2] *Ibid.*, pp. 25–76.

[3] See *The Dead Sea Scrolls Bible: The Oldest Known Bible Translated for the First Time Into English,* translated and with commentary by Martin Abegg, Jr., Peter Flint, and Eugene Ulrich (San Francisco: HarperSanFrancisco, 1999).

[4] G. L. Robinson and R. K. Harrison, "Isaiah," *International Standard Bible Encyclopedia* (Grand Rapids: William B. Eerdmans, 1982), vol. 2, p. 900.

[5] *Ibid.*

[6] For a more detailed study of the unity of the book, see Robinson and Harrison, pp. 896–902.

[7] Derek Kidner, "Isaiah," *New Bible Commentary,* 21st century edition, ed. G. J. Wenham, J. A. Motyer, D. A. Carson, R. T. France (Leicester, Eng.: Inter-Varsity Press, 1994), p. 631.

[8] Brevard S. Childs, *Isaiah* (Louisville: Westminster John Knox Press, 2001), p. 4.

CHAPTER 1

"Hear, O Heavens"

The book of Isaiah does not build up gradually to its messages of warning and judgment on the two kingdoms of Judah and Israel—it hits hard immediately. "Hear, O heavens, and listen, O earth; for the Lord has spoken," the prophet declares (Isa. 1:2; cf. Deut. 32:1; Micah 6:1, 2).

Through Isaiah God announces a formal court hearing against His people.[1] The prophet acts as herald, bringing shocking charges and summoning heaven and earth to act as witnesses to the proceedings. Scripture does not tell us if Isaiah actually assembled the people of Jerusalem to present his message or whether he just gave it to friends and disciples. If he did bring the people together, did he do it in a courtyard of the Temple? Did the smoke from the altars drift lazily overhead, casting shifting shadows on those gathered below? Did the priests and Levites stand frowning as Isaiah presented his oracle from the Lord? And did the bleating of sacrificial animals punctuate the prophet's preaching?

Ancient non-Israelite nations would enlist their various gods to participate in an important event. But here, because no other deities really exist, the God of Israel calls upon the physical cosmos—which He Himself created—to serve as symbolic witness to the validity of His indictment against His rebellious people. Centuries before, the Lord had metaphoricaly summoned heaven and earth to act as witnesses to what would happen if Israel broke the covenant He had made with them by worshiping idols (Deut. 4:25, 26). Now that that situation had actually developed, God calls upon His creation to hear the details of their apostasy.

"I reared children and brought them up,
    but they have rebelled against me" (Isa. 1:2).

The prophet speaks of Israel as God's children, showing His intimate relationship with them. But they are rebellious children, a shocking concept to the biblical world. "In Israel, as in virtually all nations of the an-

19

cient world, a father possessed the power of life and death over his children. The duty of a child was to honor him (Ex. 20:12); to rebel against him, either by word or by deed, brought death (cf. 21:15, 17)."[2] The concept of God as Father was a familiar one. Even the Gentiles thought of the gods as fathers.[3] Unfortunately, the children of the God of Israel have rejected Him.

Farm animals showed greater respect than had the nation of Judah, usually referred to as Israel in the book of Isaiah. Even such lowly creatures knew where they belonged, what they should do:

"The ox knows its owner,
    and the donkey its master's crib;
but Israel does not know,
    my people do not understand" (Isa.1:3).

"Israel has less understanding of the Lord than even the most stupid of domesticated animals."[4] His people are a sinful and corrupt nation who are not only alienated from God but who actually despise Him (verse 4). The Creator of all things struggles with the fact that His own creatures reject Him, the Holy One of Israel (one of the book's favorite terms for God).

The ancients believed that the way to discipline children was by corporal punishment. An ancient Egyptian proverb said a schoolboy's ears were on his back—that he would listen to what his teacher told him only through the use of a wooden rod on his body. But God did not want to have to teach through harsh discipline. "Why do you seek further beatings?" (verse 5), He asked in frustration and sorrow. But they seemed determined to inflict even more suffering upon themselves, until they were one mass of festering wounds (verses 5, 6).

Israel was a sinful nation and deserved rejection. It was a concept even their pagan neighbors could understand. The eighth-century Myth of Erra and Ishum described how the gods had destroyed cities because their inhabitants had spurned justice, committed various atrocities, and involved themselves in all kinds of wicked schemes. Sadly, Israel was not much different than its pagan neighbors.

Isaiah served as a prophet during a time when the Assyrian Empire was reviving from a period of dormancy and was again sweeping across the ancient Near East. Now Assyria let nothing stop its advance. It used systematic violence and cruelty as psychological weapons to intimidate anyone tempted to resist. Assyria was the original terrorist nation. When its armies invaded a country, they destroyed everything. Ancient warfare was slash and burn.

Because of the problems of supplying armies over long distances, at a time when few roads existed and pack animals and small carts or wagons were the only way to haul things, invading military forces had to feed themselves on what they could capture from the local farmers. The soldiers had to live off the land as they marched across enemy country. Aliens would literally devour Israel's land (verse 7).

People barely survived from one harvest to another. If they lost their crops to marauding armies, they would die of starvation, or of disease resulting from their weakened condition. The invading armies might burn unharvested fields or stored grain to weaken any resistance against them. And the local inhabitants might destroy their own crops and stores of food in the desperate hope that the enemy would then be unable to feed themselves and be forced to retreat. In either case, Israel would find itself in a terrible situation. Such military incursions left the landscape desolate as the enemy torched city after city. One Assyrian king, Sennacherib, claimed in a cuneiform document named by scholars the Taylor Prism to have overwhelmed 46 fortified places as well as numerous smaller settlements. His forces carried off 200,150 people and countless herds of cattle.

The repeated invasions left God's "daughter Zion" "like a booth in a vineyard, like a shelter in a cucumber field" (verse 8). Jerusalem, symbolized here by Zion, the name of the mountain it stood upon, would become as desolate as the little huts that farmers erected each year to live in while they guarded their crops, then abandoned after the harvest. If God had not left at least a few scattered survivors, Judah would have vanished off the face of the earth as utterly as had ancient Sodom and Gomorrah (verse 9).

False Worship

The reference to the two wicked cities whose depravity had forced God to destroy them triggers a new train of thought in Isaiah's sermon. Speaking for God, the prophet thunders, "What to me is the multitude of your sacrifices?" (verse 11). The Lord has told His spokesperson to announce to the people that He is tired of their Temple offerings—He finds no "delight" in them (verse 11). (The book of Isaiah will use the key term *delight* often in later chapters.)

Who asked you to bring them? He demands (verse 12). Go away; stop trampling the courtyards of My Temple, He insists.

Because the people of the ancient world considered temples to be sacred places, they carefully guarded all access to them. To use such sacred

21

space for any other purpose than worship was to profane it. Thus to trample the courtyards of a temple was to dishonor its holy nature deliberately. God's people were trying to manipulate Him for their own purposes. In His mind such motivations made their rites of worship just as sacrilegious as to use the Temple for unholy actions.

God said that the burning of incense was an abomination to Him. Incense not only masked the stench of a sacrifice; it was supposed to please and pacify the gods. But the incense the priests offered in the Jerusalem Temple could not hide the rank odor of Israel's apostasy and rebellion.

The Lord stated that He could not endure their observance of new moon festivals, Sabbath, and other religious convocations (verse 13). In fact, He hated them—they exhausted Him (verse 14). Yet God Himself had established the new moons and other religious feasts. He intended that the celebrations would bring the people closer both to Him and to each other. But, like the sacrifices and offerings, Israel and Judah had warped them to their own evil purposes. The religious events had become just one more method of manipulating God, and the people as a whole, in His name.

Even when the people stretched out their hands in prayer they offended Him. Raised hands had become the ancient Near Eastern symbol for prayer. Archaeologists find it engraved on stele and other objects. To place a carving of raised hands, or a sculpture of a person with upraised hands, in a temple or worship site symbolized continuous intercessory prayer. But when the people of Israel raised their hands in prayer, God could see only the blood that stained them—blood that stood not just for their religious hypocrisy but also for the social and economic injustice that marred the land. He found Himself turning away and refusing to listen (verses 14, 15). Their incessant prayers grated on His nerves.

Isaiah's message must have shocked the people. After all, God had instituted and commanded such religious observances. The phrase "come to appear before me" (verse 12) may, in fact, describe any form of worship.[5] Was the Lord rejecting everything He had once requested from His people? Some commentators have argued that God was doing exactly that. They point to Amos 5:22-27 and Jeremiah 7:21-23 to support their claim. But that is to miss the point here. Isaiah's message is not a new one. Centuries before, Samuel had spoken for God: "Has the Lord as great delight in burnt offerings and sacrifices, as in obeying the voice of the Lord?" (1 Sam. 15:22). The God of Israel was more concerned about why His people worshiped than how. Consider, for example, the practice of offering sacrifices.

The people of the ancient Near East considered sacrifices as meals for the gods, and temples as houses for the deities. The gods, they assumed, were dependent upon human beings for food and shelter, so humanity had leverage with them. If the gods did not do what people wanted, their worshipers could withhold the sacrifices, and the deities would go hungry until they complied with what the human beings asked for. Some of this mentality had crept into the thinking of Israel and Judah. God's people began to think that their sacrifices obligated the Lord in some way. But the God of Israel did not need human beings to feed Him. Nor did He want His worshipers to attempt to bribe Him in order to get their way. Most of all, He did not want them to use worship as a way to hide their abuse of their fellow human beings.

The clue to understanding God's rejection of Judah's worship appears in Isaiah 1:16 and 17:

> "Wash yourselves; make yourselves clean;
>   remove the evil of your doings from before my eyes;
> cease to do evil,
>   learn to do good;
> seek justice,
>   rescue the oppressed,
> defend the orphans,
>   plead for the widow."

Kidner observes that "these searching demands prepare for the offer of unmerited salvation which immediately follows."[6]

For the prophets, true religion was ethical, not just a matter of proper ritual. Even the Gentiles recognized that justice was vital to any civilized society. The people of the ancient Near East believed that the gods had the responsibility of maintaining justice. In fact, justice was part of the very fabric of the cosmos. It was external to the gods and a higher power even than they were, and thus they had no choice but to uphold it.

True Religion

The religion of Israel and Judah, however, saw the relationship of God and justice from another perspective. The Israelite worldview considered justice as part of the very character of God Himself. It was not just something He was responsible for enforcing. The people of Mesopotamia "had the spiritual obligation to please the gods. This was accomplished primarily by rituals but also by not rocking the boat of civilization. Israelites had the spiritual obligation to be Godlike. This was accomplished by ethical

23

behavior and personal holiness. Mesopotamians would have viewed the washing in physical terms accomplished through ritual. Israelites were to accomplish it in spiritual terms through repentance and reformation."[7]

For the God of Israel, true religion was to "learn to do good, seek justice, rescue the oppressed, defend the orphan, plead for the widow" (verse 17). The orphan and the widow were people with no surviving family to support them during a time when individuals could survive only by belonging to extended families. If someone had no biological family, the larger community was expected to care for them (Ex. 22:22; Deut. 10:17-19; 14:28, 29; 24:17-21). God did not want people scrupulous only in how they performed their religious rituals, but men and women who took care of each other and reflected the loving nature of their God. Biblical religion is not just what we think—it is how we act—specifically, how we treat others. Thus the prophets spent most of their time upholding social justice, because social justice is a barometer of the moral life. As Watts observes: "That which brings displeasure to God is not the sacrifice. . . . The failure to accompany sacrificial and festal worship with a lifestyle of justice and righteousness is the problem. The latter invalidates the former."[8]

Kaiser sees such acts of worship as insulting God "because their only purpose is to shield men against God's claim upon their whole life."[9] He goes on to point out that "sacrifice, worship and prayer only keep their true sense as long as in them men are really concerned to encounter the holy God. If man tries to make use of them to give himself security in the sight of God, then they become a blasphemy; sacrifice becomes a means of self-justification, the celebration of feasts the occasion of mere emotional exaltation, and prayer a meaningless, craven, or hypocritical wailing."[10]

God's people have been meticulous in their worship rituals if in nothing else. But the only way the Lord can help them is to lead them to see their condition. "Come now, let us argue it out," He challenges them (Isa. 1:18). The Hebrew verb *yakah,* translated "reason" in the King James Version, often appears in a legal context, as when presenting a case in court (as in Isaiah 2:4). Here God calls His people to the bar of divine justice. Kaiser points out that God is not mocking His self-righteous nation. The emphasis is not on their need for cleansing, but on His ability to actually do it.[11]

Modern commentators focus on the color red itself, seeing it as the hue of sin. But that may be missing the point. The dyes that produced such reddish colors were the most permanent then available, and thus difficult to remove. Yet God could completely bleach them away. He could remove any stain. And interestingly, God says that He will make His people like snow and wool. Snow and most wools are naturally white and do not require bleaching. In the words of Motyer: "The promise, therefore, is of a new, holy nation, not just the cleansing away of the past."[12] Israel will be a new creation.

But Israel must make a decision—it must let God do what needs to be done. If His people will, they will "eat the good of the land" (Isa. 1:19), but to continue to rebel will lead to death by the sword (verse 20).

Next Isaiah breaks into a funeral lament over Jerusalem (verses 21-23). God's daughter, Zion, has become a harlot, though she was once a place of righteousness (verse 21). The pure silver of her past has become dross (verse 22), and the city's leaders have become "rebels" and "companions of thieves" (verse 23). Again God, through the prophet, zeroes in on the issue of social justice by citing specific examples: the Lord's people are not protecting the defenseless orphans and widows (verse 23). They accept bribes and kickbacks and distort justice to the advantage of a few.

But God will not give up. He takes the initiative and announces His intent to purge the city of its evil. The Lord especially focuses on the failings of two groups. The counselors aided the king in developing and implementing national policies, and the judges originated and enforced law, but both classes have perverted their responsibilities. God will replace them with others who will restore justice and righteousness (verse 26). Jerusalem will return to its former character.

Canaanite religion considered trees and stones as places where the gods could dwell, and people worshiped at such sites. The practice had infiltrated Israelite religion (Jer. 3:6-9). Sacred tree symbols even appeared in the precincts of the Temple in Jerusalem. The people of Judah, after carefully offering a proper sacrifice at the Temple, might then worship at one of the fertility religion's high places. But after God purified the land, His people would be ashamed that they had ever tolerated such practices—even worse, actually "delighted" in them (verse 29).

The book of Isaiah frequently follows a pattern of alternating warnings of judgment with descriptions of what God promises His people if they will but repent and return to Him. He holds out a wonderful future for Jerusalem. It will be the center of a kingdom that will attract people from all nations to its God as the Lord brings peace to the earth (Isa. 2:2-4). But Israel must turn away from its failings or suffer the consequences (Isa. 2:5-3:26). After another description of the glory that could be Jerusalem, employing imagery borrowed from the tabernacle in the wilderness wandering (Isa. 4:2-6), God sets up another judgment scene (Isa. 5:1-7). He presents His case against Israel through the metaphor of an unfruitful vineyard. Through it He reminds them of all that He has done for them.

Parable of the Vineyard

The limestone strata of Palestinian hillsides naturally erode into terraces. Taking advantage of this, the Israelite farmers cleared the rocks from the hillsides and piled them into retaining walls to prevent more erosion and to hold in moisture during the dry season. Then they deposited soil behind the walls and leveled the terraces. The unlimited supply of stones provided building material for the huts and watchtowers the farmers would stay in while protecting the vineyards just before harvest. Still other rocks could be used to construct wine presses and cisterns.

During the growing season the farmers had to hoe constantly around the vines to prevent weeds from smothering them. Ancient Israelites did not train the vines on trellises or supports but let them trail along the ground, making them more vulnerable to weeds. Such weeds would suck the moisture out of the ground, causing the grape crop to be small and sour.

God took faithful care of His vineyard to make sure it would be fruitful. But to His great disappointment, it yielded only wild grapes. The Hebrew word for such grapes means "stinking things." In His grief and frustration God asks Jerusalem and Judah—the vineyard itself—to judge between Him and the disappointing vineyard. "What more was there to do for my vineyard that I have not done in it?" He asks (verse 4). He had gone to unusual efforts, even erecting a permanent watchtower instead of the usual temporary hut (verse 2).

The vineyard has produced a crop fit only for destruction. He expected justice, but saw only bloodshed (a wordplay, since in Hebrew "justice" is *mispat* and "bloodshed" is *mispah*). Instead of harvesting righteousness, He heard only cries of distress ("righteousness" is *sedaqa* and "cries of distress" is *seaqa*).

Feeling that He had no choice, God said He would remove the vineyard's hedge and protective wall and abandon it to briers and thorns. Not only would He no longer cultivate it, He would even command the clouds not to rain on it anymore. God does not explain the meaning of the story. It was obvious. Israel could choose to be fruitful—or be destroyed. Jesus reworked this striking imagery into His parable of the wicked tenants (Matt. 21:33-41) and perhaps saw in it the inspiration for His parable of the laborers (Matt. 20:1-16).

[1] Other court scenes include Isaiah 5:1-7 and 43:8-13, 22-28.

[2] Otto Kaiser, *Isaiah 1-12: A Commentary* (Philadelphia: Westminster Press, 1972), p. 7.

[3] *Ibid.*, pp. 7, 8.

[4] B. S. Childs, *Isaiah,* p. 17.

[5] John D. W. Watts, *Isaiah 1-33,* Word Biblical Commentary (Waco, Tex.: Word Books, 1985), vol. 24, p. 21.

[6] D. Kidner, "Isaiah," p. 634.

[7] John H. Walton, Victor H. Matthews, and Mark W. Chavalas, *The IVP Bible Background Commentary: Old Testament* (Downers Grove, Ill.: InterVarsity Press, 2000), p. 585.

[8] Watts, p. 20.

[9] Kaiser, p. 16.

[10] *Ibid.*

[11] *Ibid.*, p. 17.

[12] J. Alec Motyer, *Isaiah: An Introduction and Commentary* (Downers Grove, Ill.: Inter-Varsity Press, 1999), p. 47.

CHAPTER 2

"Woe Is Me!"

Uzziah had a long reign (perhaps part of the time as coregent with his father, Amaziah, as well as his son, Jotham) that Edwin Thiele calculated as extending from 792 to 740 B.C.[1] Archaeologists have found his name on a seal from Tell Beit Mirsim, making him one of the limited number of Judahite kings documented by extrabiblical evidence. During most of this period the Assyrians were weak, torn by internal struggles. In this power vacuum both Judah and Israel were able to expand. Uzziah extended Judahite control westward into Philistine territory and southward into Arab domains. He fortified Jerusalem and built extensively in the south, including the Negev. The prosperous condition of the nation allowed him to support a standing army.

Unfortunately, the king's successes went to his head. The rulers of many of the surrounding nations also served as chief priests of the national gods, and Uzziah apparently attempted to follow their example. He entered the Jerusalem Temple to present an incense offering. But that was a direct violation of Numbers 16:40. When Azariah and 80 other priests protested his action, Uzziah became angry. At that moment the skin on his forehead broke out in some kind of skin disease that Scripture labels under the general classification of leprosy. Whatever the condition was, it made him ceremonially unclean, and he could no longer even be in the Temple precincts. Until his death he had to live in isolation, and his son, Jotham, had to take charge of the government (2 Chron. 26:16-21).

The superscription to the book in Isaiah 1:1 suggests that Isaiah might have served as prophet during the reign of Uzziah, perhaps during the period Jotham assumed the role of coregent because of Uzziah's leprosy (2 Kings 15:5). Most Bible readers assume that Isaiah did not receive his divine call until the experience of chapter 6. The passage does not explicitly say that his prophetic ministry began then. But whether it was his initial calling, a rededication and reconsecration, or a shifting of focus from the king to the people as a whole,[2] Isaiah would give a message that would last until the end of time.

Most scholars place Uzziah's death in 739 B.C., a significant turning point in the history of the ancient Near East. Assyria now began its national revival, and in 740-738 B.C. Tiglath-pileser III made his first military campaign toward the west. Assyrians would dominate the Near East for more than a century. During that period the Neo-Assyrian Empire would destroy the northern kingdom of Israel as well as many cities and towns in the southern kingdom of Judah.

It was at this momentous time that Isaiah dates his call from the Lord to be His prophet.

"High and Lofty"

The prophet declares that he "saw the Lord sitting on a throne, high and lofty" (Isa. 6:1). But what does it mean that he "saw" God? Interestingly, the only thing that Isaiah describes is the hem of the Lord's robe. Most likely that is all he perceived of a deity whom Scripture usually regards as invisible (Col. 1:15; 1 Tim. 1:17; cf. Rom. 1:20). God never shows Himself directly. He usually reveals Himself through His actions or some symbol. The Lord let Moses see only His "back" (Ex. 33:20-23). No sinful human being can see God face to face and live (verse 20). Here in Isaiah 6 the hem of God's robe, the presence of beings known as seraphs, and the shaking of the Temple and the smoke indicate the divine presence. Some see the vision as depicting the Jerusalem Temple, others as taking place in heaven. Or it could have begun in the earthly Temple and then transferred to a heavenly scene.

As we shall observe again and again throughout the book of Isaiah, the visions and messages that God sends often employ imagery and concepts familiar to people of the ancient Near East. Even God's people knew many stories, ideas, and symbols that were widespread among the Gentiles. By using them, God could also communicate to pagan cultures, though He would alter them to fit biblical theology. Here the word translated "train" or "hem" in English refers to the hems of the garments worn by people of high rank, such as priests or kings. Ancient Near Eastern wall and seal carvings portray such garments. A fringe of three- or four-inch-long tassels decorated the hem near the ankles, and the edge of the cloth was embroidered. Isaiah's vision has the Lord's robe flowing down from His lofty throne, thus symbolizing His infinite dignity.

29

The Gentiles also thought of their gods as sitting on thrones in their temples. One northern Syria temple at Ain Dara had three three-foot-long footprints carved in the limestone slabs that lined the floor of the portico. The footprints indicated the god's presence in the temple. A stele had the relief of a deity sitting on a throne. Now all that remains of the carving is the feet extending below the hem.[3]

Seraphs stand around the high throne in Isaiah's vision and call to each other:

"Holy, holy, holy is the Lord of hosts;
    the whole earth is full of his glory" (verse 3).

The threefold repetition emphasizes that God is the ultimate form and source of holiness. Hebrew use doubles a word to indicate either a superlative or a totality, but only here does the Old Testament employ a word three times for emphasis, "as if to say that the divine holiness is so far beyond anything the human mind can grasp that a 'super-superlative' has to be invented to express it and, furthermore, that the transcendent holiness is the total truth about God."[4] The Hebrew for the "of hosts" could also be translated "surrounded by hosts." Herbert sees "glory" as representing God's "manifestation in history and nature,"[5] that is, what He does in the visible world for His creation.

The seraphs, or seraphim, are supernatural beings, but the vision may have depicted them in a way more familiar to the prophet, perhaps even somewhat like the depictions used by surrounding cultures. God always has to translate the reality of the supernatural world into something we can grasp, even though it might be quite different from ultimate reality. So far the vision has likened God to a human king in an earthly throne room. The same principle might apply to the seraphs. Scripture refers to the serpents that plagued Israel in the wilderness as seraphs (Num. 21:4-9). Elsewhere Isaiah mentions flying serpents (Isa. 14:29; 30:6). The image of winged serpents was especially common in Egypt, usually with either two or four wings. On the other hand, the vision may have presented the seraphim in human form. A relief from Tell Halaf, dating from approximately the time of Isaiah, depicts a human-shaped figure with six wings.[6] The meaning of the word suggests that the seraphs are glowing beings of light, perhaps with wings of flashing lightning.[7]

"A Man of Unclean Lips"

God's presence causes the Temple to shake and smoke to fill it. Smoke and earthquake in the Bible are common symbols of a theophany, or manifestation of God's presence (Ex. 19:18; Ps. 104:32; 144:5; cf. Ex. 40:34; Num. 9:15; 12:5; 1 Kings 19:11).[8]

The encounter with the seraphs and the powerful sense of divine holiness stuns the prophet. The people of the Bible believed that no one could see God's glory and live (Gen. 32:30; Ex. 19:21; 33:20; Judges 6:22, 23; 13:22). In the vision even the seraphs cover their eyes in God's presence (Isa. 6:2). "Woe is me!" Isaiah declares. "I am lost, for I am a man of unclean lips,[9] and I live among a people of unclean lips, yet my eyes have seen the King, the Lord of hosts!" (Isa. 6:5). The prophet is intensely aware of the fundamental difference and gulf between sinful human beings and the holy God of the universe. Isaiah identifies himself with God's fallen people of Judah and their rebellious condition.

A seraph picks up a glowing coal from an altar and flies to Isaiah. The touching of Isaiah's lips with the burning coal would be an understandable concept to the people of the time. Even non-Israelite rituals would involve purification of the lips as a symbol that the person as a whole was being purified. Diviner priests would have to undergo such purification before they could report what they had witnessed when appearing before the divine council.[10]

The seraph, after pressing the coal to Isaiah's mouth, declares, "Now that this has touched your lips, your guilt has departed and your sin is blotted out" (verse 7). The verb for "blotted out" here, sometimes translated "atonement," appears in ancient Akkadian ritual texts that describe the "wiping" away of ritual impurity of the mouth. Babylonian incantation texts frequently speak of fire as a purifying element.[11] But the people of Judah would understand the symbolism in a fuller sense, because in Scripture fire represented "the active, even hostile, holiness of God (Gen. 3:24; Num. 11:1-3; Deut. 4:12, 33, 36)."[12]

Commentators differ as to whether the altar was that of incense or sacrifice. Motyer suggests the latter, saying, "This, however, was fire from the *altar,* the place where holiness accepted, and was satisfied by, the death of a substitutionary sacrifice (Lev. 17:11). The *live coal* thus encapsulates the idea of atonement, propitiation, satisfaction, forgiveness, cleansing, and reconciliation."[13]

As mentioned, God always employs concepts, images, and symbols familiar to His audience. And whenever possible, He selects those that will speak to as wide a group of people as possible. The symbolic action here also parallels the sacrifice needed for the high priest to enter the Jerusalem Temple.

Now cleansed from sin, Isaiah hears God speaking. "Whom shall I send,

31

and who will go for us?" Instantly the prophet replies, "Here am I; send me!" (Isa. 6:8). Elsewhere the messenger God employs would be a supernatural being (see 1 Kings 22:19-22). But here God dispatches a human being.

And the message the prophet must deliver is a startling one (Isa. 6:9, 10). It would make him in many ways a prophet of sorrow. Usually we think of the joy inherent in Isaiah's promises of restoration and of the coming Messiah. But the realization that many in Israel would reject the divine message must have stunned him, flooding him with an almost overwhelming grief. How could he not be filled with sorrow when so many would refuse to listen to the good news of all that God longed to do for them?

Childs observes that the assignment that Isaiah receives is to declare to Judah, " 'Keep hearing, but do not understand. Keep seeing, but do not perceive.' Beyond this, the specific role of the deliverer of the message is spelled out. He is to dull their minds, stop their ears, and plaster over their eyes, unless by seeing, hearing, and comprehending, they might actually repent and be saved. The prophet is to be the executor of death, the guarantor of complete hardening. His very proclamation is to ensure that Israel will not turn and repent." [14] All this lest they "turn [15] and be healed" (verse 10).

Not only did God's mission for Isaiah shock the prophet; it greatly disturbs us. How could the God who sent His Son to die for and to save all human beings (John 3:16) set out here to deliberately harden the hearts of His own people? The concept is not limited to the Old Testament. We find an echo of it even from the lips of Jesus. He told His disciples that they had been given the "secret of the kingdom of God," but to those outside their circle everything would come in parables "in order that 'they may indeed look, but not perceive, and may indeed listen, but not understand; so that they may not turn again and be forgiven'" (Mark 4:11, 12).

Space does not permit us to explore this problem except to observe that a drastic situation may require a drastic approach. Part of this may involve a different way of thinking than we in the modern world are used to, or it may be God's recognition that He had to force the issue, even if it involved purging much of the people. But as we shall see, this is only a fragment of all that Isaiah would eventually proclaim. The book of Isaiah has barely begun.

The prophet's responsibility is to deliver the divine message whether or not the people accept it. If the nation does not respond, it would at least establish its clear guilt. But God keeps hoping they will return to Him. It is a consistent biblical pattern that, even after the direst warning or announcement of doom, there comes a promise of hope—of salvation. Even in this section of the book of Isaiah the darkness at the beginning transforms into singing (Isa. 12:2, 5) and salvation (verses 2, 3), and God dwells in the midst of His people (verse 6).

The prophet does not ask why God is doing so horrifying a thing. Instead he humbly inquires, "how long, O Lord?" (Isa. 6:11). How long will God abandon His people (Isa. 2:6) and hide His face from the house of Jacob (Isa. 8:17)? Is it temporary or permanent?

The Lord replies that it will continue until the "land is utterly desolate" (Isa. 6:11) and "until the Lord sends everyone far away" (verse 12). But verse 13 ends with a glimmer of hope. After a textually difficult passage, the verse ends: "The holy seed is its stump." "The tree had been felled, but its stump still stands and in the stump is the holy seed waiting to sprout in God's time."[16] The image of the stump will continue on through the book.

[1] Edwin Thiele, *The Mysterious Numbers of the Hebrew Kings* (Grand Rapids: Eerdmans, 1965), pp. 83–88.

[2] G. L. Robinson and R. K. Harrison, "Isaiah," p. 885.

[3] John Monson, "The New Ain Dara Temple," *Biblical Archeology Review,* May/June 2000, pp. 20-35, 67.

[4] J. A. Motyer, *Isaiah: An Introduction and Commentary,* p. 71.

[5] A. S. Herbert, *The Book of the Prophet Isaiah: Chapters 1-39* (Cambridge, Eng.: Cambridge University Press, 1973), p. 59.

[6] J. H. Walton, V. H. Matthews, and M. W. Chavalas, *The IVP Bible Background Commentary: Old Testament,* p. 592.

[7] O. Kaiser, *Isaiah 1-12,* p. 76.

[8] Darkness and earthquake accompanied Christ's death on the cross (Matt. 27:45-52). Both were symbols of God's near presence, but Jesus, caught up in the horror of bearing humanity's sin, felt abandoned by the Father (verse 46). An earthquake also occurred during Christ's resurrection (Matt. 28:2).

[9] Lips were the part of the body he would use to worship (speaking praise) the Lord.

[10] Walton, Matthews, and Chavalas, p. 592.

[11] *Ibid.*

[12] Motyer, p. 72.

[13] *Ibid.*

[14] B. S. Childs, *Isaiah,* p. 56.

[15] The Hebrew word "carries a double meaning in the context. It may mean 'repent,' but may also mean 'return.' The latter would specifically apply to the exiles who return to Palestine" (John D. W. Watts, *Isaiah 1-33,* p. 76).

[16] Childs, p. 58.

CHAPTER 3

A Sign From the Lord

The political intrigues and shifting alliances of the ancient Near East were just as complex and confusing as those in the geopolitical world of today. As the Assyrian threat began to loom on the international horizon, a number of the Syro-Palestinian states started forming coalitions to resist the reviving empire. Apparently Ahaz was either pro-Assyrian or at least neutral. Rezin, king of Aram (referred to in Assyrian documents as Raqianu and probably a translation of the Aramaic name Radyan), had probably been involved in installing Pekah on the throne of the northern kingdom. Now, most likely wanting to remove a potential danger to the anti-Assyrian coalition, Rezin decided to enlist the help of the northern king in an invasion against Jerusalem. Scholars have concluded that the Damascus ruler and Pekah intended a regime change, replacing Ahaz with someone more favorable to their cause. Kings were going to war, and Judah would be their victim.

Interestingly, 2 Kings 15:37 states that the Lord stirred up Rezin and Pekah to attack Judah. Was God using drastic measures to highlight Ahaz's need for help that only Yahweh could provide?

Although the two kings marched to Jerusalem, they did not seem able to sustain a siege (Isa. 7:1; 2 Kings 16:5). Still, the fact that Rezin and Pekah had formed an alliance thoroughly demoralized Ahaz and his people, perhaps because Judah had already suffered defeat from Edom (2 Kings 16:6) and the Philistines (2 Chron. 28:18), as well as raids from the Syro-Israelite coalition (Isa. 7:5-7). Their hearts "shook as the trees of the forest shake before the wind" (Isa. 7:2).

From 2 Kings 16:7 we learn that Ahaz decided to seek assistance from Assyria. He eventually sent a message to Tiglath-pileser, saying, "I am your servant and your son.[1] Come up, and rescue me from the hand of the king of Aram and from the hand of the king of Israel, who are attacking me." Ahaz was making himself a vassal king and submitting tribute money (verse 8).

Perhaps in their moment of desperation, God must have thought, Ahaz and the people of Judah would return to Him. The Lord sent Isaiah and the prophet's son, Shear-jashub (whose name embodied the divine promise "A remnant shall return"), to meet the king at the end of the conduit of the upper water storage pool in the city (Isa. 7:3). Apparently Ahaz was inspecting Jerusalem's water supply in case of a siege. He was preparing the city to resist through its own strength. While the king would probably have received the prophet at the palace, God wanted the encounter to take place at the pool, with its implied symbolism of self-defense. The Lord hoped that Ahaz would realize that Jerusalem's true and only strength rested in divine power. The prophet's son with his symbolic name was also a witness from God to the king. Most likely the king knew what the boy's name was and meant.

Isaiah had a divine message for his ruler: "Take heed, be quiet, do not fear, and do not let your heart be faint because of these two smoldering stumps of firebrands" (verse 4). Instead of a blazing inferno, ready to consume Judah, the two kings were really little more than a bit of smoke, ready to be extinguished.

Probably the royal messenger to Tiglath-pileser had not left for Assyrian territory. It was not yet too late to stop the dangerous alliance. But would the king respond to the divine plea?

The rulers of Syria and Israel might have been plotting to replace Ahaz with a puppet king named Tabeel (Isa. 7:5, 6).[2] But the Judahite king should not worry, because the attack would not happen (verse 7). Instead, the two nations would themselves be destroyed (verses 8, 9). Assyria would crush Syria in 732 B.C., strip Israel of its northern territories by at least that date, and totally destroy what remained in 721 B.C. Eventually Assyria would deport much of Israel's population and bring in foreign settlers. "Within 65 years Ephraim will be shattered, no longer a people" (verse 8).

Neither Israel nor Damascus would outlast their revolt against Assyria. "If you do not stand firm in faith," God challenged the king, "you shall not stand at all" (verse 9). Only as long as Judah relied on God could it survive. It came into existence through divine intervention and power, and it would continue only through God's strength. Faith here involves a decision to trust God and accept His leading. Such faith is concrete, not a spiritual abstraction. Ahaz must let God save his nation, not try to rescue it through human efforts.

To encourage the fearful king, the Lord declared, "Ask a sign of the

Lord your God; let it be deep as Sheol or high as heaven", (verse 11). The sign from "Sheol" would not involve calling up the dead, which Israelite religion forbade, but an earthquake or similar phenomenon. And one from the heavens might be lightning, thunder, rain out of season, or such.

The sign could be as astounding or as difficult as Ahaz wished. But the king refused the divine offer, replying, "I will not ask, and I will not put the Lord to the test" (verse 12). The king phrased his response in a way that would not openly offend the religious element, those loyal to the Lord and His prophet. "Behind the smooth scriptural talk . . . lay a plan to outwit his enemies by making friends with the biggest of them (cf. 2 Kings 16:7-10)."[3] Ahaz clearly wanted to avoid a sign. If it materialized, it would put him in a most awkward position.

Earlier, God's people had frustrated Him by constantly demanding that He prove His power, as in their continuous complaining in the wilderness. Now Ahaz rebelled in the opposite direction. He refused to allow God to prove Himself when the Lord asked the king to test His word. "It can be a sign of unbelief to ask for a sign, and it can be a sign of unbelief to refuse a sign. The criterion is whether man is ready to expose himself to the future laid down by his God and subject himself to his will."[4] Judah's ruler was afraid that God would do things in a manner that Ahaz didn't want.

The Lord was offering the king divine help. Ahaz did not so much as have to trust that it would come. God went out of His way to give Judah's leader a special token of assurance. But Ahaz rebuffed Him. "Hear then, O house of David!" the prophet announces. The phrase "house of David" was loaded with all kinds of meaning, especially the relationship established between the God of Israel and David, the founder of the dynasty. From Isaiah's reaction to Ahaz's declination of the offer of the sign it is clear that the prophet interpreted it not as piety but sheer unbelief. "Is it too little for you to weary mortals, that you weary my God also?" (verse 13). The "you" is plural. God is speaking to more than just the king. Kidner sees Isaiah as addressing the whole Davidic dynasty extending into the future.[5]

"God With Us"

Despite the king's unbelief, God would not accept Ahaz's rejection. He would keep trying to reach the king and, through him, the people of the southern kingdom. If the king would not request a sign, God would send it anyway. "Look, the young woman is with child and shall bear a son, and shall name him Immanuel" (verse 14). The birth of a child to be named "God with us" would testify that the Lord was truly with His people.

It has been said that more articles and books have been written about Isaiah 7:14 than perhaps any other passage in the Bible. The discussion centers especially on two points: Does the Hebrew phrase *ha almah* mean "a virgin," as in the King James Version of the Bible, or "the young woman," as in some more modern translations? And does the prophecy have an application in Isaiah's time, does it point only to Christ, or does it have a dual application?

The specific Hebrew word for "virgin" is *bethulah,* though *almah,* an adolescent woman of marriageable age, can bear this connotation.[6] Jewish scholars, uncomfortable with the Christian use of this passage as a prediction of Christ, have emphasized particularly the fact that Isaiah does not use the technical word for "virgin." As a typical example, Slotki stresses that "it is difficult to say with certainty who was *the young woman* referred to. Chronological considerations exclude the mother of Hezekiah; and the fact that the birth (or the name) of the child was to serve as a *sign* to convince Ahaz of the certain fulfillment of the prophecy rules out the Christological interpretation that *the young woman* and *son* are identical with persons who lived 700 years later. The wife of Isaiah, a wife of king Ahaz, a woman of the royal family, or any woman in Judah may have been *the young woman* of the text."[7] The Jewish Study Bible declares that "all modern scholars . . . agree that the Heb merely denotes a young woman of marriageable age, whether married or unmarried, whether a virgin or not."[8]

A. S. Herbert comments that *almah,* like the English word, "does not preclude the meaning of 'virgin' that appears in the Authorized Version," but he feels that the normal usage of the word "would hardly suggest it." He goes on to point out that the promised sign is not the young woman, but the child who will be born and receive the name Immanuel. A Ras Shamra text found at the ancient city of Ugarit on the Syrian coast has in one oracle a striking parallel with the biblical passage. It mentions that "a young woman shall bear a son" and uses the same noun as the biblical verse. Herbert suggests that perhaps a wife of Ahaz will bear the child. His name "will give assurance of divine protection, yet since this sign has been rejected, within a few years this same divine presence will bring the disastrous subservience to Assyria."[9]

The context of Isaiah 7:14 is Ahaz's historical situation. It must have meant something understandable to the king of Judah in his concern about an immediate threat to Jerusalem. Like so many other things in the book of Isaiah, it hints at a greater reality, but it points first to the present reality, the one Ahaz, Isaiah, and their contemporaries knew.

And beyond this, we must keep in mind that our faith must not stand or fall upon signs. When religious leaders demanded that Jesus give them a sign confirming His identity, He refused to do so (Matt. 12:38-42).[10] He said that the only sign they would receive was that of Jonah. But then He stressed that the sole legitimization of His authority was the response His teaching and life aroused in the lives of those who met Him. With or without signs, our responsibility is to respond to God's call to believe and follow Him. God has given each of us far more evidence to base our faith on than Isaiah 7:14.

Just because the prophecy might have a contemporary application, that does not mean it cannot also be pointing to Christ. As we shall see throughout the book of Isaiah, we will find people, events, and things having both earthly and supernatural implications. The biblical writers were constantly taking historical events and using them to illustrate events yet to come. A human child named Immanuel does not preclude the One who would literally be "God with us."

---

[1] The Davidic king was to be the son by adoption of the Lord Himself (Ps. 2:7).

[2] Scripture does not identify Tabeel. Scholars have offered several suggestions. One is that the Aramaic nature of the name might indicate that the individual could have been a member of the royal household. Though descended from David, his mother might have been a princess from the region of Aram. Others have proposed that Tabeel was Tubail, the king of Tyre, who had already shown his loyalty to Assyria when he paid tribute to Tiglath-pileser in 738 B.C. (Walton, Matthews, and Chavalas, p. 593).

[3] D. Kidner, "Isaiah," p. 639.

[4] O.Kaiser, *Isaiah 1-12,* p. 97.

[5] Kidner, p. 639.

[6] I. W. Slotki, *Isaiah: Hebrew Text and English Translation With an Introduction and Commentary* (London: Soncino Press, 1959), p. 35. Slotki's work is part of a traditional Jewish commentary series.

[7] *Ibid.*

[8] *The Jewish Study Bible,* Adele Berlin and Marc Zui Brettler, eds. (Oxford, Eng.: Oxford University Press, 2004), pp. 798, 799. The Jewish Study Bible emphasizes the ambiguity of the sign.

[9] A. S. Herbert, *The Book of the Prophet Isaiah: Chapters 1-39,* pp. 64, 65.

[10] Jesus had to deal with His own disciples' demand for signs. When they wanted to know the sign of His coming and the end of the age (Matt. 24:3), He in essence said that the only literal sign they would see was Him showing up in the sky (verse 30).

CHAPTER 4

Seek the Living Lord

The divine prophecy delivered through Isaiah goes on to expand the significance of the child named Immanuel, "God with us." "He shall eat curds and honey by the time he knows how to refuse the evil and choose the good" (Isa. 7:15)—that is, by the time he has matured enough to make moral judgments, usually considered in Scripture times as age 13.

The reference to curds and honey begins a pattern of allusions hinting at Israel and Syria's ultimate fate. The Hebrew word employed here appears in Assyrian and Babylonian texts to indicate "ghee," a refined form of butter that does not spoil as quickly as other dairy products. Since people had not yet domesticated bees, honey came from hives of wild bees, or the term may refer to syrup made from dates or figs. Both ghee and whatever kind of "honey" it was, were substances that could be transported easily without spoiling. They would nourish those who had to live off the land instead of being able to farm it.[1] The peasants of both the northern kingdom and Syria would no longer be able to raise crops because of the devastated land.

This situation would come about within just a few years. "For before the child [Immanuel] knows how to refuse the evil and choose the good, the land before whose two kings you are in dread will be deserted. The Lord will bring on you and your people and on your ancestral house such days as have not come since the day that Ephraim departed from Judah—the king of Assyria" (verses 16, 17).

Assyria will ravage the land, as the prophetic message illustrates through a series of vivid images: wild bees settling undisturbed in their various natural nesting sites (verses 18, 19); prisoners taken into Assyrian exile and humiliated by having their hair and beards shaved (verse 20);[2] another reference to the consumption of curds and honey, food for people unable to cultivate the land (verses 21, 22);[3] and vineyards and other agricultural land reverting to briars and thorns because not enough people remain to cultivate it (verses 23-25).[4] The land will be so dangerous that people will have to go about armed (verse 24).

Some commentators see the Assyrian devastation as striking only the northern kingdom, others Judah as well. Isaiah 8:8 has Assyrian forces invading Judah. No existing records indicate that Tiglath-pileser campaigned against the southern kingdom during his 734-732 B.C. incursion into Syro-Palestine. Either the documents perished, or the verse refers to the later invasions by Sargon or Sennacherib.

The Prophet's Son a Sign of Assyrian Invasion

In Isaiah 8:1, 2 God tells the prophet to take a large tablet (some scholars see it as a large cylinder seal[5] or even a sheet of papyrus[6]) and write on it, "Belonging to Maher-shalal-hash-baz" (a name meaning "the spoil speeds, the prey hastens"). The tablet will be a public document. Then he has it witnessed by a man named Uriah (perhaps the high priest Urijah) and another named Zechariah son of Jeberechiah. Earlier Isaiah had forced Ahaz to be a witness (whether he wanted to or not) to the sign represented by the birth of Immanuel. Now the prophet compelled two individuals who probably belonged to Ahaz's corrupt government to validate the new sign. They would be able to vouch for when Isaiah had made the predictive document—that it had not been written after the fact.

"The spoil speeds, the prey hastens," the prophet called his son every day. A plunderer would come—the king of Assyria. And he did. Tiglath-pileser invaded Israel in 733 B.C. In his records he declared, "Bit-Humria [Israel] . . . [with] all its inhabitants (and) their possessions I led to Assyria."[7]

After preparing the tablet, Isaiah went to his wife (described as a "prophetess," a term used to indicate an actual woman prophet) and "she conceived and bore a son" (verse 3). Afterward God instructed the prophet to name him after the phrase he had inscribed on the document, telling him, "For before the child knows how to call 'My father' or 'My mother,' the wealth of Damascus and the spoil of Samaria will be carried away by the king of Assyria" (verse 4). The recording of the child's name before his birth represented an enacted prophecy. It would be fulfilled quickly—even before Isaiah's son could learn to say his first words.

Judah had trembled before the danger posed by Aram and Samaria, but that was nothing, the Lord declared to Isaiah, compared to the threat from Assyria. Rezin and Pekah were like a gently flowing stream, but "the mighty flood waters of the [Euphrates] River, the king of Assyria," would be a raging torrent that would sweep over the southern kingdom (verses 6-8). Kings would go to war, and everyone would suffer.

But Judah would not totally perish. A remnant would survive. A group would remain loyal to God. A child had been named "God is with us." Now the prophet applies the truth embodied in that name to his people and nation (verse 8). All the nations might band together to attack them, but their plan would fail—because "God is with us" (verses 9, 10). And "God is with us" must become the people's motto if they are to be saved. Even more than a motto, it must be the foundation of their lives.

As for Isaiah himself, he should not fear what frightened his people. He should not become obsessed with external threats. "Do not call conspiracy all that this people calls conspiracy," God instructed him, "and do not fear what it fears, or be in dread" (verse 12). The Rezin/Pekah conspiracy was not the one the prophet should worry about. The greatest danger lay within Israel itself. The only way to avert that was for the nation to return to its God. "The Lord of hosts, him shall you regard as holy" (verse 13). The only being they should really fear was Him—"let him be your dread" (verse 13). The fear of God is a positive thing, banishing all other fear.

If God's people would come back to Him, He would "become a sanctuary," but if they will not let Him be that, then He will be "a stone one strikes against; for both houses of Israel [the northern and southern kingdoms] he will become a rock one stumbles over—a trap and a snare for the inhabitants of Jerusalem. And many among them shall stumble; they shall fall and be broken; they shall be snared and taken" (verses 14, 15). God could be either a rock of sanctuary or a rock of tripping. It all depends on how the person responds to Him. The people could either wait in hope with the remnant (verse 17)—those who accepted the promise inherent in the names Isaiah gave his children (verse 18)—or continue in their rebellion and apostasy, and perish as a result. The New Testament would later apply the imagery of this passage to Jesus (Matt. 21:44; Luke 20:18; Rom. 9:32; 1 Peter 2:8).

The Lord had given Isaiah a divine message. Using the imagery of tying a string around a scroll and sealing the knot with a lump of clay, or of depositing the scroll into a clay jar and sealing the lid, the prophet described how he shared the prophetic teaching with his disciples (verse 16). They would preserve and testify to its truth, just as an intact seal in his time indicated the authenticity of a document.

After he had passed on the divine message, Isaiah waited for God to fulfill His word. "See, I and the children whom the Lord has given me are signs and portents in Israel from the Lord of hosts, who dwells on Mount Zion" (verse 18). The prophet had told God to send him as His witness (Isa. 6:8). Now he, with his children, stand as living words of God among the people of Judah. His children's names point to the looming fall of Israel and Damascus. Beyond that, they remind Judah of its own impending judgment. The people of Judah can be part of that group that will survive all the destruction if they repent—or they can be wiped out like the northern kingdom. The decision is up to them.

But the Lord of hosts is to be Judah's source of assurance and knowledge. They should listen to the prophetic word of the living God, not the "chirp and mutter" that results from trying to consult the dead (verses 19, 20). The cult of the dead was rampant throughout the ancient Near East, and it had long fascinated many of God's people. Besides the biblical evidence of prophet after prophet protesting the practice, archaeologists have found standing stones (massebot) dedicated to the dead, and channels cut into the rock of tombs for the giving of food and drink to the deceased ancestors. But, Isaiah emphasized, seeking help from the dead would lead only to gloom and despair (verses 20-22). They needed divine teaching instead of gibberish.

Ahaz's New Altar

The Lord had promised Ahaz and Judah through the birth of one child named "God with us" (Immanuel) and another named "the spoil speeds, the prey hastens" (Maher-shalal-has-baz) that He would continue to be with His people if they would only remain with Him. But the king ignored the offer of the prophetic signs. He made an alliance as a vassal with Tiglath-pileser, bribing him to attack Damascus and relieve the pressure on Judah. The Assyrian ruler killed Rezin and marched the city's inhabitants into captivity (2 Kings 16:7-9). To pay the tribute to Assyria, Ahaz had to plunder the Temple, the royal treasury, and the wealth of his officials (2 Chron. 28:21).

After the fall of Damascus, Ahaz traveled to the conquered city to reaffirm his submission to the empire and join in Tiglath-pileser's victory celebration (2 Kings 16:10). While there, Ahaz became impressed with an altar he saw and had Uriah, the high priest in Jerusalem, build a replica for the Temple and put it in place of the Temple's bronze altar (verses 10-14). No surviving archaeological evidence indicates that the Assyrians forced their vassals to adopt the worship of Ashur, their chief god.

The rites Uriah conducted on this new altar were traditional Israelite ones (verses 12-15). But if nothing else, it implied a rejection of some elements of the Temple. And Ahaz was willing to experiment with non-Israelite religion. The king had Baal images cast, presented offerings in the valley of Hinnom, had his sons pass through fire (a pagan ritual), and "sacrificed and made offerings on the high places, on the hills, and under every green tree" (the sites of folk and fertility religion) (2 Chron. 28:2-4). He also sacrificed to the gods of Damascus, reasoning that since they had earlier helped Aram defeat Judah, perhaps if he worshiped them they would come to his aid (verse 23). He overlooked the fact that Assyria had destroyed Damascus and thus by ancient Near Eastern belief the kingdom had been defeated by the Assyrian god. In addition, Ahaz eventually closed the Temple, destroyed its ritual objects and furniture, and erected altars and worship sites (open-air shrines) throughout the land (verses 24-26).

When he finally died, the people refused to bury him in the royal tombs (verse 27).

---

[1] J. H. Walton, V. H. Matthews, and M. W. Chavalas, *The IVP Bible Background Commentary: Old Testament,* p. 593. Kidner sees the curds and honey as "enigmatic," "symbols of natural plenty (cf. Isa. 7:22; Ex. 3:8) yet also of a land depopulated (Isa. 7:22b) and untilled (cf. verses 23-25)" (D. Kidner, "Isaiah," p. 639).

[2] The Assyrians used "barber" as a divine title, though here the God of Israel does the barbering. The Hebrew word employed in the passage suggests that only the forehead was shaved. Mesopotamian culture would shave off half the hair as a humiliating punishment (Walton, Matthews, and Chavalas, p. 594).

[3] Note the tiny size of the herd of animals a person has. Other commentators have interpreted the tiny herd as being especially bountiful, thus allowing the survivors to feast on curds and honey. See, for example, B. S. Childs, *Isaiah,* p. 68.

[4] Wandering cattle would trample the cropland soil, and sheep grazing would defoliate it. The unprotected soil would erode away, destroying the carefully maintained agricultural land.

[5] Walton, Matthews, and Chavalas, pp. 594, 595.

[6] D. Kaiser, *Isaiah 1-12,* p. 110.

[7] *Ancient Near Eastern Texts,* ed. J. B. Pritchard (Princeton, N.J.: Princeton University Press, 1955), p. 284.

CHAPTER 5

The Shoot of Jesse

Isaiah 8 ends with the curse of gloom proclaimed on those who attempted to consult with the dead, but Isaiah 9 holds out hope even for
those who bear the brunt of the Assyrian invasion. Earlier Isaiah had predicted the fate of the northern kingdom, but now God declares through
His oracle that someday there no longer would be gloom for those in an-
guish. They have been brought into "contempt"; then in the "latter time"
He would "make glorious the way of the sea, the land beyond the Jordan,
Galilee of the nations" (Isa. 9:1). The people of the former kingdom of
Israel would go from judgment to redemption.

The tribal territories of Zebulun and Naphtali—including Galilee—suffered first from the Assyrian invasion of 733 B.C., perhaps within only
months of Isaiah's encounter with Ahaz at the pool. The Assyrians occupied
all of Israel except the Ephraim Hills. The three campaigns of Tiglath-pileser
III that year turned Galilee of the Gentiles into the province of Magiddu
(Megiddo), the "way of the sea" into the province of Du'ru (Dor), and the
region along the Jordan into the province of Gal'aza (Gilead).

God promised that despite their present condition all three administra-
tive areas would someday become "glorious" (verse 1). The part of Israel
first to fall would be the first to see the glory, but Galilee would eventually receive the greatest honor. In the Old Testament only Isaiah refers to
the region as Galilee of the nations, perhaps from its significant Gentile
population. It would become the earthly home of the soon-to-be
promised Wonderful Counselor, the one who would be the Messiah. In
Christ's time and for centuries afterward it would have Palestine's major
Jewish and Jewish-Christian populations.[1]

The people of Israel would find themselves forced to walk in deepest
darkness, but then they would see a great light. They would rejoice as at
harvesttime or when distributing the booty captured during a successful

military campaign. Food in the ancient world was always scarce, but at harvest people would have more of it than during any other season of the year. All ancient cultures had harvest celebrations to celebrate the fleeting abundance and the possibility of survival to the next harvest. Foodstuffs and goods were always in short supply. One of the temptations for going to war was that people could capture gold and silver and other metals, clothing, and many other things they might not be able to purchase even if they could afford them. The prophet is not condoning war but using the excitement of sharing its plunder as a concrete illustration of the joy people would feel as God began to redeem Israel.

Israel's oppression would be shattered, just as when Gideon freed the north by attacking the Midianite camp at Jezreel (verse 4; see Judges 6; 7). Although the defeat of the Midianites had taken place some 500 years earlier, God's people still remembered it as their history's most striking example of how God could deliver His people despite overwhelming odds.

"Wonderful Counselor"

Isaiah now presents perhaps the most memorable prophecy in all of Scripture.

> "For a child has been born for us,
>> a son given to us;
> authority rests upon his shoulders;
>> and he is named
> Wonderful Counselor, Mighty God,
>> Everlasting Father, Prince of Peace" (Isa. 9:6).

The prophet probably does not present a series of names, but one single name composed of all these elements. The names of people in the ancient Near East were frequently a whole sentence or phrase expressing some belief or desire.[2]

"Wonderful Counselor" indicates that God will guide this king—He will not need outside advisors, as human rulers and even the pagan gods depend on. "Wonderful" has connotations of "supernatural," as we see in Judges 13:18. Isaiah 28:29 describes the Lord as "wonderful in counsel, and excellent in wisdom." "Prince of peace" echoes "The Lord is peace" of Judges 6:24.

The final name was especially significant during a time when God's people endured constant wars, but it has even deeper implications, because "for the Israelites, peace was more than the absence of war or the continuation of war by other means; peace is a term for the condition in which all things, human beings, animals and plants, follow their destiny undisturbed. Thus it exists only when all creatures recognize God in his deity and live and act accordingly."[3]

The name of the Child affirms God's nature and power. It was a promise of things to come. Again Isaiah's language wants to burst the boundaries of this world and explode into a supernatural realm. Both God's people and Gentiles would understand the message of this prophecy. The ancient Egyptians and Mesopotamians sometimes "prophesied" about some king who would bring wondrous changes. A Babylonian document from about 1100 B.C. called the Marduk Prophecy tells about a ruler who would rebuild temples and reform society. He would establish prosperity and stability. The king would so please the gods that the deities would permanently open the gates of heaven and channel peace and justice through his rule. The Marduk Prophecy was most likely propaganda put out after the fact by a Babylonian ruler to legitimize his reign, but Isaiah's prophecy looked forward to the future and to someone greater than any human king.

An oracle from the time of the Assyrian king Ashurbanipal has the hungry being fed, the naked clothed, and prisoners set free. And Assyrian documents even describe Tiglath-pileser as the shoot or scion of the city of Baltil, who would bring justice to his people.

The promised king's authority grows continually[4] and the peace He establishes will be without end. The new Davidic king will reign "with justice and righteousness" (Isa. 9:7). The passage "closes with the fervent prayer that the Zeal of Yahweh of Hosts may do this. The invocation of the old battle name for God recognizes that this is possible only with the kind of miraculous intervention that brought Israel through the Reed [Red] Sea, brought down the walls of Jericho, and devastated the Midianite hosts before Gideon."[5]

Judgment on Israel

Isaiah now swings back to warning and judgment. The prophet tells how God sent His warning to the northern kingdom. But instead of repenting, it deliberately rejected the divine word of warning and threatened judgment. In fact, in their pride and arrogance they said, "Let it happen. So what?"

Many in Palestine built with sun-dried mud brick and roofed the structures and framed the doorways with sycamore wood. The sycamore fig was a shrublike, fast-growing tree that produced soft wood. But the people of Judah in their "pride and arrogance" decided that if invaders damaged anything, they would rebuild with expensive dressed or cut stone and costly imported cedar, making the structures even finer than before. They were oblivious to the fact that God would destroy the buildings completely because of His judgments on their sins.

To punish Israel, God would raise enemies against the northern kingdom. Both the Arameans attacking from the east and the Philistines from the west would devour the nation "with open mouth" (verses 11, 12). Interestingly, Canaanite documents describe Mot, the god of death, as having a huge mouth that could swallow everything. One lip is on the earth, the other in the heavens. His appetite is insatiable, and even the gods fear him.[6] Since the Old Testament also employs the imagery of death gulping down the living (Job 18:13, 14; Hab. 2:5; cf. Ps. 141:7; Prov. 1:12; 27:20; 30:15, 16; Isa. 5:14), both God's people and the surrounding nations could understand and appreciate Isaiah's prophecy. The Lord wanted all to understand what He was doing. But despite the raids of the Syrians and the Philistines, Assyria would still be Israel's greatest enemy.

The whole nation was corrupt, from its leadership (Isa. 9:15, 16) to the disadvantaged (verse 17), "for everyone was godless and an evildoer, and every mouth spoke folly" (verse 17). Using the image of wildfire exploding through the dry thickets and scrubby forests of Palestine, the prophet describes how the northern kingdom's wickedness would destroy it. Their evil would cause them to turn upon each other (verses 18-20). Perhaps, because of the starvation caused by the destruction of crops and military siege, they even succumbed to the horror of cannibalism.[7] But regardless of even that, Israel thoroughly deserved God's wrath. They had so persisted in their rebellion and apostasy that they had long passed the point of no return and had lost any possible desire to repent. God could not save them, because they did not want to be saved.

As we have pointed out previously, a true biblical prophet was a nation's conscience, protesting social injustice of any kind. Isaiah lists some of the crimes that Israel had indulged in (Isa. 10:1, 2). Punishment would result from what they had done to the oppressed and disadvantaged, and they would not be able to escape it (verses 3, 4). The rod of Assyria would smash their arrogance and conceit, their apostasy and deceit.

But even though God employed the Assyrian Empire as His agent of punishment, that did not give it free reign to inflict its legendary cruelty. Assyria was attacking from its own motivations. God may incorporate what people and nations do into His own plans, but they are still responsible for *why* they may do something. The Lord might allow an evil nation to punish another, but it will still face judgment for the evil reasons behind those actions. The Lord recognized that Assyria waged war for its own nefarious purposes (verses 5-12). Eventually God would deal with Assyria, because He is the true ruler of history and all nations (verses 12-16). Even Assyria would have no power if He did not permit it (as Jesus reminded Pilate, the representative of the Roman Empire [John 19:11]).

Even though God might have to destroy Israel (or any other nation, for that matter), it did not mean that everything was hopeless for the people of the northern kingdom. In Isaiah 10:17-19 God returns to the imagery of Isaiah 9:18, 19. Fire not only destroys; it purifies. Hopefully the disaster of the Assyrian invasion will teach many the folly of using the rod of Assyria as a staff to lean on, as a source of political and military support. Instead, those who had learned the lesson that God sought to teach them would "lean on the Lord, the Holy One of Israel" (Isa. 10:20). A remnant of them would return to the land (verse 21). All the destruction they went through would turn out in the end to be righteousness (verse 22). The raging flame of the Assyrian devastation would burn away all the "thorns and briars" that had once choked out "the glory of [God's] forest and his fruitful land" (verse 18).

God now gave Israel hope by bringing to their memory images from its past history. The Assyrians may beat them with a rod, as the Egyptians had done to their ancestors (verse 24). But God would shift His anger from them to the arrogant empire (verse 25). He would deal with the tyrannical Assyrians as He had the Midianites (through Gideon) (verse 26). These historical allusions not only direct Israel back to God's acts in the past, but also point to the future. When He lifts His staff over the sea in a repeat of what He did during the Exodus from Egypt (verse 26), He is promising to inaugurate a new exodus.

Isaiah expanded and intensified the new exodus image in Isaiah 11:15, 16—God's people would cross the Euphrates River on foot as they had done long ago at the Red Sea. Instead of escaping Egypt, they will leave Mesopotamian captivity (Isa. 35:1-10; 48:20, 21).

The remnant will at first be a scattered one. Assyria used large-scale population resettlement to keep nationalism from creating opposition in the territories it conquered. The empire deported the leaders, craftspeople, and other segments of captured populations to distant lands, where they would be surrounded and outnumbered by other peoples. God would have to bring His dispersed children from the far corners of the earth (Isa. 11:11, 12). After their experience in exile, the remnant would be a transformed people. No longer would Israel or Judah fight each other, but they would occupy the land and remove their enemies (verses 13, 14).

A New Davidic King

But before that could happen, the King predicted in Isaiah 9 would have to come to set up His kingdom.

Isaiah 10 ends with God in a forester motif, clearing the way for the Lord by bringing the mighty low and chopping down the tallest trees (Assyria) (verses 33, 34). Then the prophet both extends and modifies the imagery by declaring:

"A shoot shall come out from the stump of Jesse,
and a branch shall grow out of his roots" (Isa. 11:1).

Isaiah now picks up on the holy seed in the stump mentioned in Isaiah 6:13.

The Promised One would be another David, just as the original David was a shoot of his father, Jesse. The literal house of Judah might be destroyed, but that did not mean that God's promise to David (1 Chron. 17:11-14) had become void. Instead, "just as David was once chosen in a truly miraculous way from the insignificant family of Jesse (cf. I Sam. 16.1-13; II Sam. 7.18) to receive the highest honour, once again a new shoot will spring up from the root stump of the family, a second David (v. 1). Just as the spirit of Yahweh once rested upon David (cf. I Sam. 16.13; II Sam. 23.2f) the second David will also be equipped for his office by the spirit, which will bring about agreement between the will of God and that of the king (v. 2)."[8] It is a promise grounded in divine action rather than human pride or claim to royal position.

Unfortunately, some missed the divine element in this passage. They interpreted it in a way that would lead to the expectation of a warrior Messiah like that of His ancestor David. By New Testament times God's people longed for a Messiah who would overthrow the yoke of the occupying Romans. After all, one can read many of the Old Testament prophecies, especially those in the book of Isaiah (Isa. 9:6, 7; 11:1-5; 63:1-6) from this perspective. Jesus had to deal with the concept of a military Messiah even among His closest disciples. They could not understand that He would conquer, all right—but through His own death. His battlefield was the cross. God had decided to follow a different course, fulfilling the prophetic promise in what was for them a most unexpected way. As we shall see later, God is the one who makes history and fulfills His prophecies (see Isa. 9). He has the right to modify His plans to meet new situations.[9]

Both Israel and Judah had had long and bitter experiences with corrupt kings. The most important responsibility of a king in the ancient world was to establish and maintain justice, as we see in both Scripture (for example, see the prayer in Psalm 72:1, 2 and the case study of Solomon in 1 Kings 3:16-28) and texts surviving from the non-Israelite world. Gentile rulers often proclaimed what they considered to be their success in the realm of justice. "The wisdom of a king was assessed by the brilliance of his insight into complex cases, and his suitability for the throne was evaluated by his commitment to provide for the vulnerable classes of society. The ability to resolve difficult cases was believed to be divinely endowed . . . and therefore was not dependent solely on the evidence that could be presented in court (see Prov 16:10)."[10]

Most of the kings since Solomon had been anything but divinely endowed. But the shoot "from the stump of Jesse" would have the divine Spirit. He would be a wiser judge than even Solomon.

"He shall not judge by what his eyes see,
    or decide by what his ears hear;
  but with righteousness he shall judge the poor,
    and decide with equity for the meek of the earth;
  he shall strike the earth with the rod of his mouth,
    and with the breath of his lips he shall kill the wicked" (Isa. 11:3-5).

Not only would the new King bring justice, but the world itself would be radically different. Predation would cease in the animal world; and children would not have to live in fear of dangerous creatures (verses 6-9). Verses 6-9 echo the longing of many in the ancient world. At least as far back as Sumerian times the myth of Enki and Ninhursaq had depicted a marvelous world in which lions did not kill or wolves prey on lambs.

As so often throughout the book of Isaiah, the words of chapter 11 point to something more than the present existence. They break down the boundaries between the world of humanity and the realm of the supernatural and the divine.

After all this has happened, God's people would be able to burst into praise (Isa. 12:1-6). The previous chapter had an exodus allusion (Isa. 11:16), so now we find an echo of the Song of Moses (cf. Isa. 12:2 with Ex. 15:2). Not only would they thank their Redeemer, they would proclaim to the nations of the world what He had done for them (Isa. 12:3, 4).

"Sing praises to the Lord, for he has done gloriously:
    let this be known in all the earth.
  Shout aloud and sing for joy, O royal Zion,
    for great in your midst is the Holy One of Israel" (verses 5, 6).

---

[1] The Hebrew word translated "Galilee" is not a proper noun; it simply means "district." The translators of the Septuagint rendered it Galilee. Anson Rainey sees the "way of the sea" as referring to the region between the Golan and the Mediterranean Sea and north of Galilee. Jesus was active in this Gentile area (see, for example, Matthew 15:21; 16:13). He manifested Himself as Messiah in this "way of the sea," the route Assyria used as it invaded Syria. Sadly, the pagans responded to Jesus better than some of His own people (Anson F. Rainey, "Milestone From the Via Maris," a paper read at the Society of Biblical Literature annual meeting, Atlanta, Georgia, Nov. 24, 2003).

[2] Kaiser, however, sees it as a list of names paralleling the fivefold throne names of Egyptian kings, with the fifth name lost (O. Kaiser, *Isaiah 1-12,* pp. 128, 129).

[3] *Ibid.,* pp. 129, 130.

[4] Perhaps in the sense of His rulership of the earth steadily expanding as Israel evangelizes more and more of the world. See the prophetic scenario discussed in chapter 13 of this book.

[5] John D. W. Watts, *Isaiah 1-33,* p. 135.

[6] Theodore J. Lewis, "Mot," *Anchor Bible Dictionary* (New York: Doubleday, 1992), vol. 4, pp. 922-924.

[7] Seventh-century Assyrian treaties often contained curses that mentioned cannibalism against those who might rebel.

[8] Kaiser, p. 157.

[9] For a most helpful discussion of how God fulfills prophecies, see Jon Paulien, *Meet God Again for the First Time* (Hagerstown, Md.: Review and Herald Pub. Assn., 2003), pp. 22-75, and *The Deep Things of God: An Insider's Guide to the Book of Revelation* (Hagerstown, Md.: Review and Herald Pub. Assn., 2004), especially chapters 2 and 8.

[10] J. H. Walton, V. H. Matthews, and M. W. Chavalas, *The IVP Bible Background Commentary: Old Testament,* p. 600.

CHAPTER 6

The King of Babylon

In many ways Isaiah's oracle against Babylon is surprising because the city was not yet a threat to God's people. During the second half of the eighth century Babylonia was just a part of the Assyrian Empire. Sargon II and Sennacherib had established the largest political structure or network the ancient Near East had yet seen. For a time the Assyrian Empire would include even Egypt. Babylon was just another nation state overwhelmed by Assyrian military strength. Most in Judah and Israel would have regarded Assyria as their only danger—not Babylon.

But Babylon was a restless vassal, either breaking into open military revolt or trying to organize political alliances against Nineveh. One such delegation would visit Hezekiah in an attempt to enlist his support, a story told in Isaiah 39, 2 Kings 20:12-19, and 2 Chronicles 32:31. (We will discuss the incident in more detail in the next chapter.) Merodach-Baladan, who sent the emissaries to Jerusalem, ousted the Assyrian rulers from Babylon at least twice. But God, through His complete understanding of the political currents of the ancient Near East, knew that Assyria would eventually self-destruct and that Babylon, and later the Medes, would gain control. And, as we shall see in the case of Cyrus of the Medo-Persian Empire, the Lord would direct those evolving historical events.

In the time of Isaiah, Babylon threatened Judah primarily through the danger of entangling the southern kingdom in the nationalistic schemes of Merodach-Baladan. Later, though, it would become Jerusalem's greatest external danger.

Isaiah's oracle against Babylon divides into seven sections: (1) the gathering of the army of the Lord of hosts (Isa. 13:1-5); (2) a declaration of the impending day of the Lord (verses 6-18); (3) the destruction of Babylon (verses 19-22); (4) Israel's salvation (Isa. 14:1, 2); (5) a taunt of Babylon's king (verses 3-21); (6) a second description of the destruction and devastation of Babylon (verses 22, 23); and (7) a prophecy dealing with the doom of Assyria, Babylon's overlord during Isaiah's time (verses 24-32).

Although the oracle is addressed to Babylon, it is rather general in nature, and aside from the reference to Babylon in the heading (Isa. 13:1), verse 19 is the only mention of the city by name in the rest of the chapter. The day of the Lord is depicted as a de-creation of the earth. The oracle picks up imagery from Genesis 1 and turns it on its head. The sun, moon, and stars cease to give light (Isa. 13:10). The reference to the failing light of the heavenly bodies may be a multifaceted allusion. Besides worshiping them as gods, the Babylonians also believed that their movements were omens for earthly events. Astrology was rampant in Mesopotamia. If anything happened to these astronomical objects, it would undercut the Mesopotamian worldview.

Not only would the heavens be de-created, but human life, the ultimate stage of Creation, would become almost extinct (verse 12). Both the heavens and the earth will convulse, imagery that the Old Testament writers will continue to expand (Hag. 2:6) and the New Testament will identify with the last days (Luke 21:26; Rev. 6:12-17).

God will stir up the Medes against Babylon (Isa. 13:17), the city will vanish like Sodom and Gomorrah (verse 19), and the land will become desolate and inhabited only by wild animals (verses 20-22). Babylon will become a wilderness, a desert.[1] The Egyptians and other peoples of the ancient Near East considered deserts and uninhabited lands as regions of chaos.[2] God would de-create Babylon and return it to a level of primeval chaos, much as the world had been before God began to create in Genesis 1.

The Downfall of the King of Babylon

Chapter 14 begins with God restoring Israel to the Promised Land. But they will not come back alone. Others, attracted to Israel's God, will attach themselves to the house of Jacob. They want to identify with—to become part of—the people of the God of Israel. Israel will now rule over those who once held them captive. Many from the other nations will now be Israel's slaves (Isa. 14:2). The God of Israel and Judah will become the God of the nations. It is a theme that will grow and intensify throughout the rest of the book of Isaiah.

The prophet now has a special message for Babylon, the city and empire that in the Old Testament became the symbol of Israel's captivity and exile. The redeemed people of God, the prophet announces, will someday be able to taunt the king of the empire that had once conquered and enslaved them. "How the oppressor has ceased! How his insolence has ceased" (verse 4). Isaiah then goes on to describe the fate of the king of despotic Babylon. The prophet depicts him as plummeting to Sheol (the domain of the dead) and making his bed among the maggots and worms (verses 9-11). His fall will be so complete and dramatic that the whole world can but only marvel (verses 16-20).

The prophet declares:

"How you are fallen from heaven,
    O Day Star, son of Dawn!
How you are cut down to the ground,
    you who laid the nations low!
You said in your heart,
    'I will ascend to heaven;
I will raise my throne
    above the stars of God;
I will sit on the mount of assembly
    on the heights of Zaphon;
I will ascend to the tops of the clouds,
    I will make myself like the Most High.'
But you are brought down to Sheol,
    to the depths of the Pit" (verses 12-15).

Whom is Isaiah talking about? A human ruler? A supernatural being? Or both?

Commentators and theologians have traditionally interpreted verses 12-15 as referring to Satan. Modern scholars tend to see the king of Babylon portrayed here strictly as a human being.

Isaiah 14 is another example of how the book keeps pointing to a supernatural dimension beyond the events and personages of this world. That human conflict reflects at least dimly a vaster struggle going on in the cosmos as a whole. Yes, the prophet begins with a human ruler—but Isaiah has more in mind than just that. Clearly the center of the passage (verses 12-15) soars beyond a mere human enemy of God's people. The "Day Star" seeks a position that is not his by right. And it is more than an earthly rulership. He wants to rise to a level with the "Most High," God Himself (verses 13, 14), so that he can sit in the "assembly of the north" ("Zaphon").

As we have seen so far—and will continue to discover throughout the rest of the book—Isaiah is communicating in ways understandable both to his people and to the Gentiles. The passage employs much imagery that would have been familiar even to non-Israelites. Some of them consist of terms for the realm of the supernatural. The "assembly of the north" was the divine council. Canaanite mythology depicted El, the father of the gods, as holding the assembly of all the deities on a mountaintop, the traditional boundary between heaven and earth. "Most High" (Elyon) was not only a title for Yahweh, God of Israel; it was also a divine title (and perhaps divine name) in Ugaritic, Aramaic, and Phoenician writings about Canaanite gods.[3]

The "Day Star"[4] longs to be like God, but in his hubris he destroys himself. Instead of rising to the utmost heights, he is brought down to Sheol, to the pit. His fall is so spectacular it is as if he becomes an abandoned corpse, cast aside like garbage, dumped in a pit and left for scavengers (verses 15–19).[5] The biblical world considered not being buried properly one of the most shameful things imaginable. "For the people of the ancient world there was no more terrible fate than to remain unburied, and no more sacred duty than that of giving burial to relatives or comrades in arms."[6] The king's fate stands in shocking contrast to his dream of seizing power. Instead of being entombed in a royal sepulcher, he rots with the dogs and other carrion.

Some scholars have tried to see this passage as just an allusion to some Canaanite tale in which a lesser god by the name of Day Star tries to sit on the god Baal's throne in the north, but the deity's legs are so short his feet cannot reach the throne's footstool. One suggestion has been a Ugaritic myth about a god named Athtar. The god attempts to rule during Baal's absence, but he does not do so out of any spirit of rebellion. Instead, Athtar eventually receives rulership over the earth or underworld. His name does mean "Shining One, Son of Dawn," though.[7]

Other scholars have seen parallels between the Isaiah 14 passage and an ancient document called the Myth of Anzu. In it a combination lion and bird creature seeks to gain power over the other gods by stealing from the chief god, Enlil, the Tablets of Destinies that the Canaanite pantheon employs to govern the world. Anzu declares a series of "I will" statements that echo those of the king of Babylon. "I myself will take the gods' Tablet of Destinies," Anzu announces. "The responsibilities of the gods I will seize for myself. I will establish myself on the throne and wield the decrees. I will take command over all the Igigi-gods."[8]

But none of the possible parallels reflect all the details of Isaiah 14. While no exact counterpart to the king of Babylon appears in ancient Near Eastern literature,[9] the biblical author seems to be employing an image that would be familiar to the people of Israel as well as to non-Israelites. He wants to identify the king of Babylon with the concept of a cosmic rebel.[10] The behavior of the Babylonian ruler mirrors the greater evil of the first being that attempted to usurp divine power.

Gregory A. Boyd sees Isaiah as depicting both a human king and the supernatural dimension behind him. "Earthly battles correspond to heavenly battles," he observes. The king of Babylon is "a participant in and a prototype of a much vaster drama of another oppressive conqueror who attempted to set up an illegitimate kingship on a cosmic scale."[11] He goes on to point out that "when we consider the cosmic dimension of the mythological motifs Isaiah was alluding to in this passage, the later church tradition seems quite justified in identifying Helel ben-Shahar . . . with Satan. In its own fashion, the story of the rebellious king of Babylon illuminates the story of the struggle of the rebellious king of the whole world."[12]

Isaiah was not the only biblical prophet to use multilevel imagery of a person who exhibits such hubris, a desire to usurp divinity. Ezekiel echoes Isaiah's depiction of a larger than human king.[13] In Ezekiel 28 he denounces another of Israel's enemies, the king of Tyre, a powerful commercial kingdom on the Mediterranean coast of what is now the country of Lebanon. Here too we find a being tempted to usurp godlike powers. And like the tyrant in Isaiah 14, he will also meet a violent fate.

But Ezekiel pushes his imagery even further into the supernatural realm. The cosmic dimension is still more dramatic. Ezekiel 28 describes someone who was "full of wisdom and perfect in beauty" (verse 12). The being had once lived in "Eden, the garden of God" (verse 13). Originally created "blameless," the garden had remained that way until infected by "iniquity" (verse 15). Because he became "filled with violence" and "sinned," God had to expel the being "as a profane thing from the mountain of God" (verse 16). As we have already noted, ancient Near Eastern thought regarded the mountain of a god as the place where the deity lived and met with the divine council, a close counterpart to the biblical concept of heaven. Thus here Ezekiel portrays God as having to cast the being out of the divine realm, for "your heart was proud because of your beauty; you corrupted your wisdom for the sake of your splendor" (verse 17).

Both Isaiah and his fellow prophet Ezekiel hint more at the source of ultimate rebellion and tyranny than they explain it. But while they do not present matters in great theological detail, their allusions to kings with larger-than-life aspects remind us that more is going on in the world than we realize. That the conflicts that trouble human history are but shadows of the greater and supernatural struggle.

The oracle now returns to the human level. In the oracle against Assyria[14] the prophet raises a theme that we will explore later—that prophecy comes to pass because God makes it happen. After speaking of the fate of Assyria, God declares through the prophet:

"This is the plan that is planned
    concerning the whole earth;
and this is the hand that is stretched out
    over all the nations.
For the Lord of hosts has planned,
    and who will annul it?
His hand is stretched out,
    and who will turn it back?" (Isa. 14:26, 27).

Scripture here employs the same imagery for both God's involvement in history and His creation of the physical universe. God "stretches His hand" to accomplish both. His guidance of history, His fulfilling of prophecy, is as much a creative act as His bringing the universe and its life forms into existence. God is the Creator of both the world and history.

Oracles to the Nations

Babylon and Assyria are not the only nations that are the subjects of prophetic messages. The book of Isaiah now presents oracles to Philistia, Moab, Damascus, Ethiopia, Egypt, and other countries. Many of these nations have injured God's people in one way or another. Some of the oracles warn of punishment for how they have treated Israel and Judah. But others hold out startling promises. In Isaiah 19, after telling of the disasters He will bring on Egypt (Isa. 19:1-17), God announces that He will make the Egyptians His people (verses 18-22). But even more amazing: not only will the Egyptians worship the God of Israel, but so will the Assyrians. People of the one nation will turn to the other to worship Yahweh together (verse 23). They will join with Israel, and God will declare, "Blessed be Egypt my people, and Assyria the work of my hands, and Israel my heritage" (verse 25).[15] In Isaiah 14:1, 2 we saw the concept of all nations worshiping the God of Israel, and it will become ever more prominent throughout the rest of the book. God has plans for a glorious future for all His people. And His goal is that all nations will become His people.

Chapters 13-23 have depicted God's concern about certain nations that have oppressed Israel and Judah. Now God expands His focus to the whole earth. In chapters 24-27 Isaiah depicts God's triumph in behalf of His people. The section is a series of poems and songs about the end-time.

First, chapter 24 reveals how God will overthrow a corrupt earth. The total devastation the Lord inflicts will touch everything—the land, nature, and society. It ignores class and position (Isa. 24:2, 3). The real cause of the desolation is that all the nations have "transgressed laws, violated statutes, broken the everlasting covenant" (verse 5). The nations may not have as full a knowledge as God's people, but all have some sense of right and wrong, and the nations have ignored or gone against it (cf. Rom. 1:18-32). They must suffer the punishment their behavior deserves (Isa. 24:6).

The grapevine, a frequent biblical symbol of joy and social pleasure, withers and dies (verses 7-11). Gloom and despair lurk everywhere, and cities lie in ruins (verses 10-12). People will flee in terror, only to find themselves in worse situations (verses 17, 18). Again we see God de-creating the earth. The author employs echoes of both the Creation account and the Flood story. (The Flood is itself a reversal of Creation, as the reader will find by comparing the sequence of creative acts of Genesis 1 with the first half of the Flood narrative. In the second half of the Flood story God re-creates the world.)[16] The windows of heaven open (verse 18), and the earth trembles and shatters (verses 18-20). Light vanishes, and darkness returns (verse 23).

Verses 21 and 22 seem to be pointing beyond the earthly situation. "The apocalyptic character of this passage makes it more likely that the author is describing the imprisonment of other powers (angels) who have attempted to rival God's power, rather than earthly kings. Certainly the pattern in much of the Old Testament is for kings to be executed (see Judg 8:21; 1 Sam 15:33) or forced to negotiate terms of surrender (2 Sam 10:19). Mesopotamian texts from Mari describe the 'imprisoning' of sacred images, as does the Cyrus Cylinder from Persian records."[17] Revelation 19:20-20:15 and Enoch 18:16 will expand on this imagery.

Again, Gentiles reading or listening to Isaiah's prophecy would have understood it. He was employing a common literary form of the ancient Near East: a lament over a devastated city. Here Isaiah applies it to the whole earth. "The litany of destruction found in this city lament parallels the style contained in the Sumerian *Lament Over the Destruction of Ur* as well as in other ancient Near Eastern expressions of grief over fallen cities. Comparisons include the descriptions of utter desolation, the fact that no person of any rank has been spared, and the failure of nature to provide what previously nurtured the people. The Sumerian lament speaks of devastating winds, drought, famine and bodies piled up in the streets unburied. The twentieth-century B.C. Egyptian *Visions of Neferti* also depicts a land laid bare and cursed by the disappearance of the sun and the drying up [of] the life-sustaining canals. The prophecies of Balaam (found at Deir'Alla and dating to 700 B.C.) describe angry gods who 'lock up the heavens,' turning every creature into a scavenger and forcing even princes to wear rags and priests to 'smell of sweat.' " [18] (Most likely the priests would "smell of sweat" because they would no longer be able to perform their ritual washings and would then become ritually unclean.)

The ancient world was thoroughly acquainted with destruction and the collapse of both society and nature. Similar images fill the media today. Even the modern secular world would acknowledge that such suffering results from what human beings have done to each other and to the natural world.

But intermingled among the depictions of gloom in Isaiah 24 are other images. In verses 14-16 we see glimpses of praise to God for what He is doing. Chapter 25 develops this theme. It is a poem of praise consisting of three sections: a hymn of praise from the prophet himself (Isa. 25:1-5); a feast that the Lord gives to celebrate His eradication of death (verses 6-8); and a hymn of praise from God's people (verses 9-12). They exalt because God has swallowed up death, the entity that the ancients visualized as swallowing up everything else. The Old Testament also personifies death (Hosea 13:14; cf. 1 Cor. 15:54, 55). Death, whom the pagan inhabitants of Palestine considered as the god Mot, is gone forever. The people proclaim, "This is the Lord for whom we waited; let us be glad and rejoice in his salvation" (Isa. 25:9).

Chapter 26 presents a three-part poem looking forward to the day when God's victory will be complete. The first section is a pilgrim's song extolling Jerusalem, the city of God (Isa. 26:1-6), the second a song of trust in God (verses 7-19), and the third a promise that God will punish evil (26:20-27:1).

In Isaiah 8:19-22 God had told the prophet of the dangers of any attempt to consult with the dead as a way to save the nation from its enemies. Now in Isaiah 26:14 Isaiah returns to the topic of the dead, declaring "the dead do not live; shades do not rise—because you have punished and destroyed them, and wiped out all memory of them." The dead could not help the nation—but God could (verse 15).

"Your Dead Shall Live"

Yet the memory of the dead of God's people is not forgotten. The Lord remembers. And the righteous dead will do more than just whisper advice, as the pagans thought. Isaiah proclaims:

59

"Your dead shall live, their corpses shall rise.
    O dwellers in the dust, awake and sing for joy!
  For your dew is a radiant dew,
      and the earth will give birth to those long dead" (verse 19).

Some have seen this passage as nothing more than an assurance that God's people will someday be resurrected as a nation, similar to Ezekiel 37:4-14. Such scholars consider Daniel 12:2 as the only clear reference in the Old Testament to bodily resurrection. But, as Motyer points out, "the (mere) continuance of the community as such does not meet the problem that the poem describes. The world has not come to new birth. The continuance of the community does nothing to solve this. Secondly, relating this passage to its parallel in [Isaiah 26:] 5-6, it is the inhabitants of the 'lofty city' who *dwell in the dust.* The Lord's people already inhabit the city of salvation ([verse] 1). It is others who need to be drawn in. In this connection *your dead* is more likely to mean 'the dead you are concerned about' and this is then capped by the Lord's claim upon them as (lit.) 'my corpses'(not as NIV), i.e., 'The dead I am concerned with.' It is, then, a promise of life for the world: the counterpart of the vision of [Isaiah] 25:6-10a. But [Isaiah] 25:7-8 looked forward specifically to the abolition of death itself. If we view [Isaiah] 26:19 in its context in this way (as indeed we must), then its terms go beyond any figurative significance to the literal sense of a full resurrection."[19] Kidner calls verse 19 "one of the two clear promises in the OT of bodily resurrection."[20]

Isaiah 26:19 provides the imagery of dew. Dew is a vital source of moisture in Palestine, especially during the dry season. Such dew, condensing out of the air during the night, revives wilted plants. But the image may have had even more symbolism. The text refers to the moisture as "your dew," God's dew. Egyptian texts describe dew as "the tears of Horus and Thoth," gods involved in the afterlife. Their "tears" contained the power of resurrection. Yahweh's dew can truly bring the dead back to life.

In Isaiah 5 the Lord had sung "The Song of the Unfruitful Vineyard." Now in chapter 27 God returns to the vineyard image.

Isaiah 27:1 is a transition between the themes of chapters 26 and 27. Isaiah 26:21 tells how the Lord will punish the earth's inhabitants for the evil they have done. The punishment will extend also to the instigator of that iniquity. The prophet employs a common ancient Near Eastern symbol of the source of chaos. In Canaanite mythology Leviathan was a monster that fought the chief gods and sought to destroy creation.[21]

Again the prophetic word uses imagery that even Gentiles could understand. "Ugaritic and Canaanite myths contain detailed descriptions of a chaos beast representing the seas or watery anarchy in the form of a many-headed, twisting sea serpent. There is a close affinity between the description of Leviathan in Isaiah as a 'coiling serpent' and the Ugaritic Baal Epic, which speaks of how the storm god 'smote Litan the twisting serpent.' In both cases there is a sense of the God of order and fertility vanquishing a chaos monster.

"Several other passages in the Old Testament mention Leviathan, but most of them, like Psalm 74:14 and Job 41:1-34, speak in terms of God's creative act that established control over watery chaos (personified by the sea serpent). In Isaiah 27:1, however, that struggle between order and chaos occurs at the end of time. It may be that the fall of Satan, portrayed as a seven-headed dragon in Revelation 12:3-9, also echoes the Ugaritic image of Litan as 'the tyrant with seven heads.'"[22]

God and His prophets may use common—even pagan—imagery, but they modify it to represent ultimate truth. The Lord can take over even pagan symbols for His own purposes, filling them with new meaning. Here Leviathan is no longer a god, or even an actual creature. He is just a symbol and must not be interpreted as anything more than a symbol. But it assures us that God is in complete control even of chaos.

"On that day" (Isa. 27:1) the Lord will punish and slay the original cause of sin. Once more the book of Isaiah points beyond the earthly conflict to the ultimate cosmic struggle. And "on that day" God will restore His vineyard as He redeems Israel. The rest of the chapter relates how He will reconstitute His spiritual vineyard (verses 2-6), contrasts His destruction of Israel's enemies with His discipline of the nation (verses 7-11), and offers a promise that He will bring back all of Israel's exiles to Jerusalem (verses 12, 13). God uses the imagery of threshing, one that the New Testament will expand in its description of the harvest at the Second Coming, especially in the book of Revelation.

---

[1] Seleucus Nicator, ruler of the Seleucid Empire, abandoned Babylon in the late fourth century B.C., establishing his new capital, Seleucia, 40 miles away. By the second century A.D. Babylon itself was totally empty.

[2] The Egyptians considered the god Seth, who struggled with his brother Horus for rulership of the gods, as the god of the desert.

[3] J. H. Walton, V. H. Matthews, and M. W. Chavalas, *The IVP Bible Background Commentary: Old Testament,* p. 604.

[4] Ancient tradition links the Hebrew word used here *(helel)* with Venus, the morning star. The Latin Vulgate translated it with *luciferos,* "shining one," the source of the name Lucifer *(ibid.,* p. 603).

[5] John D. W. Watts, *Isaiah 1-33,* p. 211.

[6] Otto Kaiser, *Isaiah 13-39* (Philadelphia: Westminster Press, 1974), p. 41.

[7] Gregory A. Boyd, *God at War: The Bible & Spiritual Conflict* (Downers Grove, Ill.: InterVarsity Press, 1997), p. 159.

[8] Walton, Matthews, and Chavalas, pp. 603, 604.

[9] Margaret Barker, "Isaiah," *Eerdmans Commentary on the Bible,* eds. James D. G. Dunn and John W. Rogerson (Grand Rapids: William B. Eerdmans Pub. Co., 2003), p. 511.

[10] Neil Forsyth, *The Old Enemy: Satan and the Combat Myth* (Princeton, N.J.: Princeton University Press, 1987), p. 138.

[11] Boyd, p. 160.

[12] *Ibid.* Boyd identifies the human king of Babylon with Sennacherib, who destroyed the city of Babylon when its former king tried to throw off the Assyrian yoke. Thus Sennacherib became in a sense an illegitimate king of Babylon. But his seeing the image of the Babylonian king as having both human and supernatural dimensions does not stand or fall with this specific identification. Although the reader will not agree with every point he makes, Boyd's book provides an excellent survey of the struggle between good and evil, Christ and Satan, throughout Scripture.

[13] Margaret Barker sees the Ezekiel accounts as the closest parallel and that Isaiah 14 reflects a Hebrew story of "someone being thrown from God's presence because of his sin or pride" ("Isaiah," p. 511).

[14] Isaiah 14:24 ("as I have planned") picks up the same Hebrew word ("intends") used of Assyria's own plans (Isa. 10:7). Human agencies may "intend," but God "plans" and over-rules. He unravels all evil schemes and weaves their threads into a tapestry of His own design.

[15] Jon Paulien suggests that Egypt and Assyria would share in Abraham's mission to the nations (*What the Bible Says About the End-time* [Hagerstown, Md.: Review and Herald Pub. Assn., 1994], p. 59).

[16] See Gerald Wheeler, *Saints and Sinners: An Insider's Guide to Bible People and Their Times* (Hagerstown, Md.: Review and Herald Pub. Assn., 2000), p. 31, and Jon Paulien, *Meet God Again for the First Time,* pp. 25, 26.

[17] Walton, Matthews, and Chavalas, p. 617.

[18] *Ibid.*

[19] A. Motyer, *Isaiah: An Introduction and Commentary,* p. 178.

[20] D. Kidner, "Isaiah," p. 647.

[21] Kidner observes that "the unusual epithets, *gliding, coiling* (or 'slippery,' 'wriggling'), are exactly the terms used of Leviathan (Lotan) in the ancient Canaanite epic of Baal, who vanquished *the monster of the sea.* This Canaanite material is reshaped to the divine truth it now conveys—truth which demolishes its pagan structure. Both here and at [Isaiah] 51:9, 10 the context is judgment, not (as in paganism) a supposed struggle in which, before he could proceed to his desired task of creating an ordered world, the creator-god first disposed of the opposition of the gods of disorder" (p. 649).

[22] Walton, Matthews, and Chavalas, p. 619.

CHAPTER 7

Tests of Faith

Beginning with chapter 36, the book of Isaiah shifts from oracle and prophecy to an interlude of history. Chapters 36–39 serve as a bridge between the largely prophetic section of chapters 1–35 and the even more extensive prophetic series of chapters 40–66. The four chapters deal with king Hezekiah and his faith in response to two threats that he recognizes (the Assyrian invasion in Isaiah 36 and 37 and his own impending death in Isaiah 38) and a third danger he does not recognize and succumbs to (the visit of the Babylonian envoys, Isaiah 39).

Earlier (Isa. 14:24–27) the prophet had predicted that eventually Assyria would endanger Judah. In fact, it would deal treacherously with the southern kingdom (21:2; 24:16; 33:1). Now it has happened. Another king has gone to war. Sennacherib's forces flood into Judah during the fourteenth year of Hezekiah's reign, approximately 701 B.C. For a time after the destruction and deportation of Israel, Judah had paid tribute to the Assyrian Empire. Inscriptions authorized by Sennacherib announce that Hezekiah turned over 30 talents of gold (an amount equal to about one ton) and 800 talents of silver (about 25 tons). Other Assyrian texts report that the king of Judah also had to send to Nineveh his daughters, concubines, musicians, ivory, elephant hides, and other tribute.

This would have been a severe financial drain on Judah's economy. One can understand why Hezekiah decided to stop paying it, a step that Assyria naturally considered an act of rebellion (2 Kings 18:7). Scripture indicates that the Lord had prospered Judah as Hezekiah faithfully obeyed God (verses 3–7). He probably felt that God would be with him if he broke the alliance with Assyria.

The Assyrian Empire operated on a policy of military intimidation. It could not permit any of its vassals to secede, lest the empire start immediately unraveling. Sennacherib had to force Hezekiah back into line. He must make the vassal king an example of what happened to those who revolted. Sennacherib had just defeated one of them, Merodach-Baladan, after a fierce two-year struggle. Now he marched against the rebels in the west. There he dealt with uprisings among the Philistines and the city of Tyre. Soon his armies penetrated Judah.

First, they systematically destroyed all the fortified cities in the outlying territory of the southern kingdom. In his official annals Sennacherib mentions 46 sites that he attacked. He was so proud of the capture of one of them, a city named Lachish, that he had depictions of the siege carved on the walls of his palace at Nineveh. Also he had a whole room devoted to storing the spoils he carried away from the city.

From Lachish, Sennacherib sent a personal delegation as well as his army to Jerusalem to demand its surrender. Hezekiah attempted to persuade the Assyrian king to pull his forces from Judah. "I have done wrong," he told the Assyrian ruler, "withdraw from me; whatever you impose on me I will bear" (2 Kings 18:14). Sennacherib demanded 300 talents of silver and 30 of gold. To pay the tribute, the Judahite king took all the silver in the Temple and royal treasury. He also stripped the gold sheathing from the Temple doors and doorposts. For a moment the Assyrian king seemed to accept the bribe and eased the pressure. But then he resumed the attack. Perhaps he asked for and took the tribute just to exhaust Judah financially so that it could not buy any allies.

The book of Isaiah ignores Hezekiah's submission as recorded in 2 Kings because it is not relevant to the prophet's theology of portraying the event as a struggle between God and the earthly kingdoms. Isaiah "wants to bring us straight to the point where he can demonstrate the effectiveness of faith, not the results of faithlessness."[1]

Challenge to Jerusalem

The Assyrian delegation that had ridden up from Lachish met with Hezekiah's representatives at the same place where Ahaz, years before, had refused to accept a sign from God that the Lord would deliver Jerusalem (Isa. 7:3). Ahaz had refused to demonstrate faith in God. Now Hezekiah was reaping the harvest of Judah's unfaithfulness. Yet God, because of Hezekiah's faith, would prevent a total destruction of Jerusalem.

The Rabshakeh, a title meaning "chief cupbearer" and perhaps here indicating a military field commander or provincial governor, delivered a speech in Hebrew, the language of the people of Judah. It stressed four themes. After declaring that Jerusalem's confidence that it could resist

Assyria was a delusion, he emphasized that Judah could expect no help from Egypt. Instead of a staff that Judah could lean on for support, the Nile kingdom was only a broken reed that would puncture the hand of anyone that tried to use it (36:6).

Egypt, although relatively powerless at the time, had sought to create a coalition among the small states of Palestine that would stand up against Assyria. A pro-Egyptian faction in Judah's government had wanted to form an alliance with the Egyptians. But, as the Assyrian official reminded the people of Jerusalem, Egypt was in no condition to aid anyone. Assyria had beaten back an Egyptian expeditionary force at Elteke. As Isaiah had already said, to ally with Egypt was to sign one's own death warrant. It was making a covenant with death (Isa. 28:15).

Second, the Rabshakeh argued, Judah could not count on its God. Strangely, the Assyrian official now points to something that Jerusalem had done right: Hezekiah had closed the high places and public altars, restricting public worship to the Temple (Isa. 36:7; 2 Kings 18:3, 4). The Assyrian leader realized that the elimination of folk religion would provoke opposition among many people. (Not all the high places involved pagan gods. Many—if not most of them—were traditional shrines dedicated to the God of Judah,[2] though they were vulnerable to syncretistic practices, mingling false worship with the true.) Shutting down the local shrines and religious sites made worship inconvenient in the countryside. The people would have to travel to Jerusalem. In addition, the old high places and shrines had a long tradition and were familiar to the people. Few things can upset religious people more than changing long-held religious routine and structure. The Rabshakeh wanted to stir up that resentment.

Next, the Assyrian representative rubbed in Jerusalem's face the embarrassing fact that even if the invaders gave Judah 2,000 horses, the tiny kingdom could not supply the men to use them (Isa. 36:8). "How then can you repulse a single captain among the least of my master's servants, when you rely on Egypt for chariots and for horsemen?" (verse 9). Judah simply had no resources to resist Assyria.

Finally, the Rabshakeh claimed that Assyria had divine authority to attack Judah. "Moreover, is it without the Lord that I have come up against the land to destroy it? The Lord said to me, Go up against this land, and destroy it" (verse 10). Apparently Assyria's spies had reported the warnings Isaiah had given to Jerusalem.

Whenever anything of interest happens a crowd gathers. The inhabitants of Jerusalem lined the city's golden-hued limestone walls, listening.

The Assyrian representative was waging psychological warfare against the Judahites, seeking to undermine their will to resist. Hezekiah's officials realized that the Rabshakeh's words were having a demoralizing impact, and they asked Sennacherib's delegation to switch to Aramaic, the international diplomatic language of the time (verse 11). (Later, Aramaic would become the common language of Palestine.)

The Assyrian official refused, and continued speaking in the language of Judah. After alluding to the horrors endured by those trapped in a besieged city (verse 12), he speaks directly to the listening citizens of Jerusalem. The Rabshakeh charges that Hezekiah will be unable to defeat the invaders, nor should the people of the city listen to the king's claims that their God will save them (verses 13-15). Instead, they should sue for peace with Sennacherib. If they were to, they could live in peace and comfort until the Assyrian king arranged to transfer them to another land. Not only would it spare them the suffering of further siege and war, but they would receive a new home much like the one they had now (verses 16, 17). Better a new home than death by starvation or the sword in their present one.

Motyer suggests that Sennacherib wanted to avoid a long war that would keep him away from the Assyrian homeland. After all, he had just put down a major rebellion in Babylon, and political opposition could emerge at any time even in Nineveh. The Assyrian field commander was trying to force surrender of Jerusalem as quickly as possible. "He makes his offer [sound] as attractive as possible: an unmolested present ([verse] 16) and an agreeable future ([verse] 17). He cannot hide the well-known policy of deportation, but he does his best to sweeten the pill." [3]

Their fate was sealed, the Rabshakeh announced. "Do not let Hezekiah mislead you by saying, The Lord will save us. Has any of the gods of the nations saved their land out of the hand of the king of Assyria? Where are the gods of Hamath and Arpad? Where are the gods of Sepharvaim? Have they delivered Samaria out of my hand? Who among all the gods of these countries have saved their countries out of my hand, that the Lord should save Jerusalem out of my hand?" (verses 18-20). The Assyrian official's speech has repeatedly used the Hebrew for "trusting." He has ridiculed everything Judah might have trusted in and raises the question "In what does Jerusalem place its trust?" It is a vital question that the people of the city must answer to decide their fate.

A widespread belief in the ancient Near East held that when countries went to war their national gods fought the gods of their opponents. One side lost because its god had been defeated by the deity of the other side. The god of Assyria, Assur, the Rabshakeh claimed, had overcome all the gods of the nations he cited. Assur would triumph over Yahweh if Jerusalem remained determined to resist. The hand of Assur and the king of Assyria were mightier than the hand of the Lord. In fact, since the God of Samaria was supposed to be the same as the God of Judah, Jerusalem's God had already failed against the Assyrians once. The Assyrian leader directly challenged the Lord.

Hezekiah's representatives, as well as the people, did not respond, because the king had commanded that they should not answer anything the Assyrian leader said (verse 21). If nothing else, their silence must have frustrated the Rabshakeh at least slightly as he stood there in his chariot. Only the rustle of harness, the squeak of a chariot wheel as a horse restlessly shifted position, broke the silence. Even today Near Eastern culture is quite open in displaying its emotions and feelings. The Assyrian officer must have wondered if his psychological tactic was getting through to the people of Jerusalem. But it had. On the way back to the palace the three Judahite officials tore their clothing, the standard biblical expression of grief (verse 22; cf. Isa. 20:2; 1 Kings 20:31; Neh. 9:1; Dan. 9:3).

Judah's king not only ripped his own clothes, but covered himself with sackcloth, an even more dramatic symbol of grief. Then he went to the Temple (Isa. 37:1). Scripture does not say what he did there, but most likely he prayed for guidance and for God to save the city. In addition, he sent Eliakim, Shebna, and the senior priests with a message to Isaiah.

"Thus says Hezekiah," they told the prophet, "this day is a day of distress, of rebuke, and of disgrace; children have come to the birth, and there is no strength to bring them forth" (verse 3). The people were paralyzed with grief and fear, and the world seemed to have come to a complete halt. The narrative implied that the three officials expected that what they told the prophet he in turn would bring to God. "First, there was an admission of failure ([verse] 3). *Distress* is the fact of adversity, *rebuke* acknowledges that the trouble was merited; *disgrace* notes the public shame which followed; and children . . . *deliver* is the frustration of all that was planned."[4]

Perhaps, the king's delegation suggested to Isaiah, "the Lord your God" had heard the challenge the Rabshakeh had brought from Sennacherib. Were they distancing themselves from Yahweh, making Him Isaiah's and Hezekiah's God, not theirs? Surely they would have believed that God could hear everything said on earth—or did they question even that? But Hezekiah's request was clear: "Lift up your prayer for the remnant that is left" (verse 4). The king had heard Isaiah's long proclaimed theme of the remnant.

In the biblical account the prophet does not need to pray. He already knows the Lord's answer. Don't be afraid, he directs the delegation to tell the king. They have nothing to fear from the Assyrian propaganda (verses 5, 6). God will drive Sennacherib away. The Lord will cause the Assyrian king to hear a rumor that will send him rushing back to Nineveh. There Sennacherib would be the victim of an assassin's sword (verse 7).

When the Rabshakeh returned to Lachish to report to his master, he discovered that the king had moved on to his next target, Libnah, eight miles northeast of Lachish and closer to Jerusalem. While he was at Libnah the Assyrian ruler's spies began to pick up reports of Egyptian military activity. "King Tirhakah of Ethiopia" was a Kushite king of the twenty-fifth Egyptian dynasty, reigning as the dynasty's pharaoh around 690-664 B.C. At the moment, however, he was not yet king and held the position of commander in chief of Egyptian forces for his brother, Pharaoh Shebitku.[5]

Under the influence of the Holy Spirit, Sennacherib took the rumor seriously. But first he tried to intensify the pressure on Hezekiah, perhaps hoping that he would surrender immediately. He needed to reunite his armies to meet the potential threat from Tirhakah. The Assyrian ruler dispatched messengers to repeat his previous warning that Jerusalem could not hope to resist the might of Assyria, but this time he directed it specifically to the Judahite king. "Do not let your God on whom you rely deceive you by promising that Jerusalem will not be given into the hand of the king of Assyria" (verse 10). Interestingly, this time the Assyrian ruler makes no reference to Judah looking to Egypt for help—only to "your God." And he expands his list of nations and national gods defeated (verses 11-13).

Total Trust in the Lord

Sennacherib's message was both oral and written. Hezekiah read the letter, then took it to the Temple, where he spread it out before God (verse 14). Unlike his predecessor Ahaz, Hezekiah decided to put his total trust in the Lord. He prayed to God for deliverance for Jerusalem. His prayer incorporated many of the themes so dominant throughout the book of Isaiah. Yahweh is the only God, as well as God of the nations. Furthermore, He is the Creator (verse 16). Hezekiah asked the Lord to respond to Sennacherib's mocking challenge against Him (verse 17). The king of Judah acknowledged that the Assyrians had defeated many nations and their deities, but such gods were not real in the first place. They were only idols made with human hands (verses 18, 19). "So now, O Lord our God," Hezekiah concluded, "save us from his hand, so that all the kingdoms of the earth may know that you alone are the Lord" (verse 20). Prove who You are by saving us, he pleaded. Sennacherib had taunted the Lord, and God must respond.

Soon Isaiah had a divine message for the king, God's reply to Hezekiah's prayer. The Lord addressed the prophetic word to Sennacherib and the Assyrian Empire.

Assyria despised and mocked Jerusalem (verse 22). By scorning Jerusalem, Assyria was really insulting Zion's God.

> "Whom have you mocked and reviled?
>> Against whom have you raised your voice
> and haughtily lifted your eyes?
>> Against the Holy One of Israel!" (verse 23).

The empire bragged about its conquests (verses 24, 25), but Assyria triumphed only as the God of Israel and Judah permitted it. No matter how chaotic it might seem, history is still under His ultimate control.

> "Have you not heard
>> that I determined it long ago?
>> I planned from days of old what now I bring to pass" (verse 26).

Assyria could devastate the nations only because God had made it a part of His working out of history (verses 26, 27). But even though He allowed Assyria to rampage across the ancient Near East, the nation was still responsible for what it did. The empire regarded the nations it conquered as nothing more than a crop to harvest (verse 27). Assyrian cruelty would not go unpunished. God would allow the empire to go only so far. And He could not ignore Sennacherib's direct attack on Him.

> "Because you have raged against me
>> and your arrogance has come to my ears,
> I will put my hook in your nose
>> and my bit in your mouth;
> I will turn you back on the way
>> by which you came" (verse 29).

In military campaign after campaign Assyria had brutally dragged its prisoners into captivity by embedding hooks in their noses. Sennacherib and his forces would receive their own heartless treatment.

God had offered signs to Ahaz of His power to control history. Now He did the same for Hezekiah. The Lord would make it clear that Sennacherib's retreat was not just a coincidence. The prophet Isaiah added a *sign,* a visible token that it was the Lord at work. For two years, owing to the Assyrian invasion, agriculture was impossible, yet the land would, of itself, produce enough until in the *third year* normal tillage could be resumed."[6]

The Assyrian advance had prevented the normal planting of crops in 701 B.C. But the grain that had naturally seeded itself[7] would supply enough food for the people to get by until the crisis passed and the farmers could resume their normal routines. Even the vineyards, which required extensive care, would produce a harvest (verse 30). God would make sure the land would support Judah, and it would be a sign that He had also repelled the invaders.

But even more than that, the unexpected harvest was a symbol of the theme of the remnant that runs like a golden thread through the fabric of the book of Isaiah. "The surviving remnant of the house of Judah shall again take root downward, and bear fruit upward; for from Jerusalem a remnant shall go out, and from Mount Zion a band of survivors. The zeal of the Lord of hosts will do this" (verses 31, 32).

As for Sennacherib, his attempt to capture the city would fail. He would not even be able to mount a siege, but would return to Nineveh (verses 33-35). One of the things that compelled the Assyrian king to retreat was a massive number of deaths among his armies. Scripture declares that an angel struck them down (verse 36). The angel might have worked through an epidemic. Gathering large numbers of people together as during a siege was dangerous. The primitive sanitation of military camps provided ideal conditions for the spread of disease. In fact, military sieges were often a race between diseases wiping out the invading armies and starvation killing the defenders. Only a part of Sennacherib's forces had surrounded Jerusalem. Bimson suggests that the high casualty figures might indicate that whatever caused their deaths had spread to the Assyrian forces elsewhere in Judah.[8]

Significantly, while the inscriptions authorized by Sennacherib claim that he "caged up" Hezekiah in Jerusalem, they do not say that he captured the city or that he even began a siege. They focus on the fact that he did stop the revolt in Palestine. He depicted the overthrow of Lachish in carved reliefs, but not Jerusalem, a far more important prize. Some scholars have suggested that his detailed listing of the tribute from Hezekiah was an attempt to draw attention away from the fact that the campaign against Jerusalem actually failed.[9]

Eventually Sennacherib found himself the victim of the ever-present danger of all ancient rulers: assassination. One day the king went to worship his god. No ancient records mention a god named Nisroch, so the biblical writer may be doing what Scripture often did—deliberately distorting the name of a pagan deity for polemical purposes. During his visit to a temple in 681 B.C. his sons Adrammelech and Sharezer murdered him with the sword, then fled to the region of Ararat (Urartu), a kingdom near the vicinity of Lake Van in what is now Armenia (verse 38). Extrabiblical records give Adrammelech's name as Ardamulissi, and the ancient Babylonian chronicle records Sennacherib's assassination and the accession of another son, Esar-haddon.

Hezekiah's Illness

In Isaiah 38:1 Isaiah came to his king with a most shocking message: Hezekiah would die.[10] The impending death was not a punishment or judgment on the ruler.[11] In fact, Scripture regarded him as an exceptionally good king (2 Kings 18:3; 2 Chron. 31:20, 21). Apparently he faced death simply because he lived in a world of sickness. We have already mentioned the constant reality that disease almost always broke out during military campaigns and sieges. Since in the parallel accounts in 2 Kings and 2 Chronicles the incident appears in the context of the siege of Jerusalem, one wonders whether some connection exists between it and his illness. Whatever the cause of the king's condition, he had a fatal disease and needed to deal with its consequences. God's command to "set your house in order" may have included the selection of a successor.[12]

Naturally, Hezekiah found his fate difficult to accept. Who wouldn't? He turned his face to the wall, a biblical phrase that can indicate displeasure and frustration (1 Kings 21:4), but whether it was a reaction of sulkiness or a desire for privacy in a world that provided little of it, the king at least prayed (Isa. 38:2, 3). "Remember now, O Lord, I implore you, how I have walked before you in faithfulness with a whole heart, and have done what is good in your sight" (verse 3; cf. 2 Kings 20:3). He used phraseology that the author of the book of Kings reserved for those whom the two books presented as the better rulers of Judah. Hezekiah did not directly ask for a reprieve, only that God not forget how he had served Him.

Was God waiting to see how the king would react to the situation? Was He seizing the opportunity provided by the disease to test Hezekiah's trust in Him? If so, that does not mean that the Lord sent the illness. The king had reaped one of the consequences of being trapped in a crowded city (people from outlying areas would have fled to it for protection from the Assyrians) and contracted the illness when an overstrained sanitation system broke down. The Lord then employed that consequence for His own purposes.

In 2 Kings Isaiah had barely left the palace before the Lord sent a message to the prophet. The book of Isaiah did not give any time frame. But both accounts related how God told Isaiah to report to the king that He had heard Isaiah's prayer and would heal him. Not only that, but He would add 15 years to the king's life (Isa. 38:5). That amount of time was equivalent to more than half a life span, for the life expectancy for most people in the ancient Near East at this period was about 20 years. (Isaiah was already 39.) In addition, God would deliver him and Jerusalem from the grasp of the king of Assyria (verse 6).

As He had done with Ahaz, God gave Hezekiah a second sign.[13] The Lord made the shadow of a sundial (most likely a stairsteplike structure) move backward 10 steps (or intervals, 2 Kings 20:9-11).[14]

Isaiah 38:10-20 consists of a hymn of praise by Hezekiah for his healing. Like many ancient rulers, the king seems to have had an interest in devotional material. Besides this poem, Proverbs 25:1 credits him with having his scribes collect and copy some of the Solomonic proverbs, and 2 Chronicles 29:30 reports that he instructed the Levites to use the psalms of David and Asaph as part of his restoration of the Temple services. Hezekiah's hymn here has some echoes of these psalms. It consists of a description of his lament (Isa. 38:10-14) and a poetic account of the Lord's healing (verses 15-20).

At first Hezekiah struggled with the fact that, at the peak of his life, he would be sent to Sheol, the realm of the dead (verse 10). If he should die, he would no longer have any communion with either God or the living (verse 11). Only the living can have any awareness of God. The king lamented his fate through a series of vivid images: the packing up of a shepherd's tent and loom and the cutting off of woven fabric from the loom (verse 12). The tearing down of the shepherd's camp and the dismantling of the loom symbolized impermanence, and the snapping of threads to remove the finished material from the loom depicted the fact that his life had now reached its completion. Also his situation reminded him of a lion mangling its prey (verse 13), and he moaned like a dove (verse 14). The king could not sleep because of his grief (verse 15). Beginning in verse 16 he asked God to restore him to health. God had forgiven his sins (verse 17), but death would halt his thanks and praise for that forgiveness (verse 18). Only the living can praise God (verse 19). By verse 20 he felt confident that God would save him from death, and he would praise the Lord in the Temple through music all the rest of his life.

Although the healing came from God, the Lord often works through natural processes, as might be the case here. The prophet Isaiah instructed the court physicians to apply a fig poultice to the boil. The brief account does not tell us whether Hezekiah had a peptic ulcer, internal poisoning, or something else. On the other hand, the application of the "lump of figs" could have been an "acted" oracle or sign. In either case, Hezekiah recovered quickly. Even though he had had a terminal illness, he became well enough to go to the Temple on the third day (2 Kings 20:5-8). And he was thankful—but not thankful enough.

Envoys From Babylon

Second Chronicles 32:25 states that "Hezekiah did not respond according to the benefit done to him, for his heart was proud. Therefore wrath came upon him and upon Judah and Jerusalem." We see his failure to appreciate his salvation in his reaction to the visit of the envoys from Merodach-baladan. Known in Assyrian and Babylonian documents as Marduk-ap-la-idinna II, this man was a Chaldean sheikh of the Bit-Yakin tribe. About 731 B.C. he joined forces with Tiglath-pileser III against another Babylonian ruler. But he was not blindly loyal to the Assyrian Empire. As mentioned previously, he revolted several times against Assyrian control. Then, in 722 B.C., after the death of Shalmaneser, he expelled Assyrian forces and ruled for 10 to 12 years until finally overwhelmed by Sargon. But Merodach-baladan did not give up. He fomented intrigue until, when Sargon's reign ended in 705 B.C., revolts sprang up in both the eastern and western territories of the Assyrian Empire.

Isaiah 39:1 reports that the restless vassal dispatched several visitors to Hezekiah after he learned through the diplomatic grapevine that the Judahite ruler had miraculously recovered from a terminal illness. The Babylonian nationalist sent a gift and letters to Hezekiah. Scripture does not reveal the contents of the letters, but from what we know of Merodach-baladan's constant plotting, they must have urged Hezekiah to join his cause. The fact that the Judahite king took the envoys on a tour of his treasury and arsenals suggests more than just that Hezekiah was proud of his wealth (verse 2). The king was showing them the financial and military resources he could contribute to the struggle.

God wanted Judah to depend upon Him, not on diplomacy, alliances, and military strength. Hezekiah was making the same mistake as Ahaz.

When Isaiah asked the king where the delegation had come from and what he had done with them, he naively told the prophet that they were from Babylon and that "they have seen all that is in my house; there is nothing in my storehouses that I did not show them" (verse 4).

The Lord had a message for the king that in some ways was even worse than the one announcing his death. Someday Babylon would come and take away all that Hezekiah had shown its envoys. "Nothing shall be left, says the Lord" (verse 6). The land would be devastated and depopulated, as had happened to the northern kingdom. As for the king himself, some of his descendants would be made into eunuchs to serve in the palace of the king of Babylon (verse 7). In a culture that regarded children as a form of personal immortality, the inability to father children would be a cruel fate. Besides that, for the children of the Davidic kings to become eunuchs would prevent the emergence of the prophesied shoot of Jesse.

Just as Ahaz had done with Assyria, Hezekiah had put his hope and trust in Babylon instead of the Lord. His nation would reap the consequences of his action. In the words of Motyer, the prophet told the king, "You want to commit all you have to Babylon, therefore all you have will go to Babylon."[15] Motyer also points out that this section has a chiastic structure that drives home its message of how the king turns from his reliance on God to reliance on the powers of this world and the consequences of this shift.

When Hezekiah was sick, Isaiah came to him, but when he was well the Babylonian envoys visited him. In both cases the king chose how he would respond, but those choices were very different, with dramatically opposite outcomes. One choice saved Jerusalem as well as the king, while the other doomed the city. The first led to life, the other death—the death of an entire nation:

A^1 (Isa. 38:1) Hezekiah faces death
   B^1 (verse 1) "Isaiah . . . came . . . [said] . . . Thus says the Lord"
      C^1 (verses 8-22) Hezekiah's dedication
      C^2 (Isa. 39:1, 2) Hezekiah's defection
   B^2 (verses 3-7) "Isaiah came . . . said . . . Hear the word of the Lord"
A^2 (verse 8) Hezekiah faces life[16]

This section goes from triumph to tragedy. Hezekiah faced death better than he would face the rest of his lengthened life.

In Isaiah 38:1 God had predicted Hezekiah's death. The king responded in a way that allowed the Lord to alter the future. But the prediction of Isaiah 39:6, 7 would not change. As Motyer observes: "The prediction in [Isaiah] 39:6 is every bit as categorical as the prediction in [Isaiah] 38:1, which was met by prayer, and divine mercy turned it into blessing. But, in the course of this chapter, works have replaced faith, man has replaced God, and pride has replaced humility. When smug self-importance replaces tears and prayer, the word of God proves its obduracy and accomplishes its grim purposes."[17]

The fact that God would have no choice but to fulfill this prediction is seen in the way Hezekiah responded to it. "The word of the Lord . . . is good," he told the prophet. And why? "For he thought, 'There will be peace and security in my days'" (Isa. 39:8). Judah's fate was the worry of future generations, not his.[18]

A terrible doom hung over Judah. It was destined for captivity in Babylon. The nation would become a people of sorrows. But God would not abandon them. He held out hope for them, as we shall see in the rest of the book of Isaiah.

---

[1] J. A. Motyer, *Isaiah: An Introduction and Commentary*, p. 222.

[2] Cf., for example, the shrine mentioned in the incident recorded in 1 Samuel 9:11-25.

[3] Motyer, p. 224.

[4] *Ibid.*

[5] Bates suggests that Tirhaka was confirmed as king of Cush and thus heir to the throne of Egypt shortly before the battle of Elteke. See Robert D. Bates, "Could Taharqa Have Been at the Battle of El Tekah?" *Near Eastern Society Bulletin* 46 (2001): 43-63.

[6] Motyer, pp. 229, 230.

[7] Perhaps from uncut grain along the edges of fields and plants overlooked by the gleaners.

[8] John J. Bimson, "2 Kings," *New Bible Commentary,* p. 381.

[9] J. H. Walton, V. H. Matthews, and M. W. Chavalas, *The IVP Bible Background Commentary: Old Testament*, pp. 406, 454.

[10] The chronology of when this event happened is vague. Since Hezekiah reigned 29 years and God promised him 15 more years of life, the incident must have taken place during the fourteenth year of his rule, about the same time as Sennacherib's invasion (2 Kings 18:2). Bimson concludes that the events in 2 Kings 20 are out of chronological order because they do not reflect favorably on Hezekiah. "They are deliberately separated from the rest in order to provide a contrast with the picture in chs. 18-19. And they are placed here rather than earlier because they provide a bridge to the reign of Manasseh and its consequences" (Bimson, p. 380).

[11] Richard Nelson, *First and Second Kings* (Atlanta: John Knox Press, 1987), p. 243.

[12] Donald J. Wiseman, *1 & 2 Kings: An Introduction and Commentary* (Leicester, Eng.: InterVarsity Press, 1993), p. 286.

[13] In 2 Kings 20:8 the ruler asks for the sign. Isaiah 38:7 presents God announcing the sign without Hezekiah requesting it.

[14] The 2 Kings account also has God giving the king a choice of the shadow either advancing or retreating the 10 intervals.

[15] Motyer, p. 233.

[16] Adapted from Motyer, p. 233.

[17] *Ibid.*, p. 242.

[18] "To Hezekiah there was comfort in postponement ([Isaiah 39:] 8); but not to Isaiah. Evidently he took this burden home with him, and so lived under its weight that when God spoke to him again it was to one who in spirit had already lived long years in Babylon ([verses] 6–7) and could 'speak to the heart' (*cf.* 40:2) of a generation of exiles yet to be born" (D. Kidner, "Isaiah," p. 655).

CHAPTER 8

The Looming Exile

Isaiah's question to Hezekiah as to the origin of the envoys who arrived after the king's healing from a fatal disease, and Hezekiah's answer, foreshadow the rest of the book. The delegation had come from Babylon, and to Babylon Hezekiah's people would go because of their continual rebellion and apostasy. Beginning with Isaiah 40, the book speaks of a future that the city will pass through and the empire that will rise and fall within that future. Babylon was the power that God alluded to (but did not name) when He called Isaiah to mission, the power that would destroy the prophet's homeland and carry off its people (Isa. 6:11-13).

In the Dead Sea scroll manuscript QIsa^a, what modern translators label as Isaiah 40:1 begins two lines from the bottom of the column in which Isaiah 39:8 ends. Thus the word of doom of Isaiah 39:5-7 and the word of comfort (Isa. 40:1) lie side by side.[1] The book of Isaiah pronounces judgment, then immediately presents a message of comfort.

Three anonymous voices or heralds proclaim that message. The first begins in Isaiah 40:1, the second in verse 3, and the third in verse 6. "Comfort, O comfort my people, says your God." In verse 2 God tells the prophet to "speak tenderly to Jerusalem." The Hebrew literally means "speak to the heart." Scripture generally uses this phrase when one is seeking to reassure a person or win back their affection (see, for example, Gen. 50:21; Judges 19:3; 2 Sam. 19:7; Hosea 2:14). As we read further into the book of Isaiah we see that "my people" are particularly those who would go into exile in Babylon. Jerusalem is doomed, but the judgment has not yet fallen, and God seeks to encourage His people as that future approaches. Their suffering will be even worse than what they have already gone through. But someday it will end. Here Jerusalem represents the exiles who will experience that captivity.

They may have turned away from Him, but He has not abandoned

77

them. God's people have to face judgment for what they have done, but in the process divine justice will be met. The "penalty is paid" (verse 2); then their relationship with God moves on to His ultimate plan. After they have served their term of suffering, they will receive "from the Lord's hand double for all [their] sins" (verse 2). At first glance the passage might seem to say that their penalty will be twice what they really deserve. But that is not what it means. "Double" "means 'to fold over, fold in half' (Ex. 26:9); the noun, as here *(kiplayim),* occurs only in Job 11:6, where divine wisdom is 'two-sided' in the sense that it always includes hidden realities beyond the reach of the human mind. So here, the thought is not of an excessive punishment running beyond what the case required, but of a dealing with sin that includes realities beyond our comprehension."[2]

We might have ideas of how we might handle sin, but we do not really understand all its implications. Only God knows how to actually deal with it. Our instant solutions would only cause more problems. Sin and its consequences are beyond human comprehension, but even more so is what God plans for His people when they return to Him.

"A Highway for Our God"

The second voice proclaims, "In the wilderness prepare the way of the Lord, make straight in the desert a highway for our God" (Isa. 40:3). The image is that of an impending arrival of an important rider. The ancients had only primitive roads. They primarily transported both people and goods on the backs of donkeys and camels. While the populace did have wheeled vehicles, they did not use them extensively. Even roads intended for wheeled transport were not paved. A few paved roads appeared during the later years of the Assyrian Empire, but the ancient Near East would have to wait until the arrival of the Romans and their military engineers before it would have a sizable system of paved roads.

Even roads used by wagons and carts were only staked out and the soil leveled. These roads were mostly along major trade routes. Erosion could quickly ruin all roads. The Assyrians expected the local population to keep them in some kind of repair. One Assyrian king, Esarhaddon, arranged a treaty with one vassal that required the local ruler to make "smooth [Esarhaddon's successor's] way in every respect."[3] Thus when royalty traveled anywhere, they expected the local inhabitants to make as passable as possible the road that the king and his entourage would use.

The prophetic oracle in Isaiah calls for a road across the desert that would require valleys to be filled in, mountains and hills removed, and all uneven ground leveled (verse 4). The imagery presents something far beyond the capabilities of ancient road builders. And even more important, it would be a processional road. A Babylonian hymn summons the worshiper of the god Nabu to make his "way good, renew his road. Make straight his path."[4]

The road Isaiah speaks of is not a military road but a supernatural one—a road for the God of the universe. Furthermore, the term *wilderness* reminds Israel of how God had led them during the Exodus, thus promising that He could do it again.

When the royalty of prophecy arrived, He would travel along that specially prepared highway and all the people would see Him (verse 5). The divine coming could not be hidden. All the earth would witness the glorious procession. And because the road had been carefully prepared, His arrival was assured. No impassable terrain, no broken wheels or axles, would stop His coming.

But He would not arrive unannounced. Verse 6 employs the image of the royal herald or messenger. In a world without newspapers, magazines, radio, or television, news spread through the aid of "criers" who would report important events, decrees, or other information. Such royal or personal messengers were used in all kinds of situations. We have already seen how the Rabshakeh came to Jerusalem to discuss surrender terms.

The crier's message is that "all people are grass, their constancy is like the flower of the field" (verse 6). Hot desert winds could instantly wither grass, flowers, and other vegetation. Such wilting or fading plants are a common biblical symbol of impermanence, of the fleeting. What the biblical writer has in mind here is difficult to determine exactly. Is it that people wilt and fade under the hot blast of spiritual testing, or is the author stressing the fleeting nature of human existence while waiting for God to fulfill His promises? Clearly the contrast is that the Word of God lasts forever (verse 8). Here the emphasis behind "forever" is permanency, the ancient Near Eastern concept of perpetuity rather than just endless days.[5] God will never change His intentions, His ultimate goals. He will keep working despite all human resistance to fulfill His promises.

The herald (either someone speaking to Jerusalem or Jerusalem itself) has commanded to go to a high and public mountain and proclaim the "good tidings" or "good news." The Greek word used in the Septuagint to translate the Hebrew for "good news" or "glad tidings" in verse 9 is the same word translated in the New Testament as "gospel."

The message is clear: "Here is your God!" (verse 9).

"See, the Lord God comes with might,
> and his arm rules for him;
his reward is with him,
> and his recompense before him" (verse 10).

Like a conquering king the Lord of Israel and Jacob will bring back the booty of His victory as rewards to His favorites—to the remnant, His faithful people.

Verses 10 to 31 are organized in a chiastic structure.[6] (We have mentioned one example already in the previous chapter. Isaiah has many of them.) We will not look at it in detail, but will mention some of the points the biblical writer seeks to emphasize by this literary device. First, it emphasizes that God comes with power (a triumphant king) and that He cares for His people. The author depicts the divine through a symbol well known to the people of the ancient Near East—the king as shepherd of his people. The concept appears in documents as far back as the time of Lugalzagessi of Sumer (c. 2450 B.C.). The Old Testament frequently employs it, and Jesus would take up the imagery in the New Testament, identifying Himself as the Good Shepherd (John 10:11). Here in Isaiah God tenderly cares for His sheep, carrying the lambs and gently leading the ewes.

The Greatness of Jerusalem's God

In Isaiah 40:12 the passage switches to the creation imagery so dominant in the book of Isaiah. God measures the universe like an architect and weighs the earth on a balance. He is so infinite that even mountains are as dust on the pans of His scale. They are so insignificant that they are not even worth the bother of blowing them off. Then verse 13 takes another common Near Eastern image and turns it on its head. The ancients believed that the gods made all major decisions in a divine council. But the God of Israel and Jacob does not need counselors to help Him figure out what He should do.

"Whom did he consult for his enlightenment,
> and who taught him the path of justice?
Who taught him knowledge,
> and showed him the way of understanding?" (verse 14).

The various images and symbols seek to communicate the incomprehensible greatness of Jerusalem's God. He is so infinite that all of the nations together are like dust on His scales, a mere drop in His bucket (verse 15). The Lord dominates all the nations. Such a magnificent God demands worship. But how do you do that? Through sacrifices? Even all the wood and animals of fertile Lebanon would not provide a sacrifice worthy of Him (verses 16, 17).

The center of a chiastic structure always contains the most important point the author wants to make. Verses 18-20 form the center of this section. Scripture asks:

"To whom then will you liken God,
or what likeness compare with him?" (verse 18).

God is beyond anything known to the human race. One thing that definitely has no comparison with God is an idol (verses 19, 20). It is a point that Isaiah makes more than once in his book.

Idols—Worthless Gods

The people of the ancient Near East did not believe that their idols were actually gods. They held that an idol was just an object that the deity temporarily occupied when the god sought to manifest itself among humanity. In both Egypt and Mesopotamia the idol was consecrated with a special ritual called the Opening of the Mouth. It gave symbolic life to the cult object and was similar to the ceremony that Egyptians believed would restore life to their mummies. People then prayed to the idol as if it were the god itself. Isaiah, as elsewhere in the Old Testament, ignores this distinction between the idol and the god that inhabited it. He sees all pagan gods as human creations and mocks pagan worship by focusing on the act of manufacturing the physical representation of the imaginary divine being.

Elsewhere the Old Testament questions the idea that human beings can even make a worthy earthly home for the true and infinite God. Solomon, during his dedication of the Jerusalem Temple, asked, "But will God indeed dwell on earth? Even heaven and the highest heaven cannot contain you, much less the house that I have built!" (1 Kings 8:27). But whether it be the god itself or a dwelling place for the god, it is ludicrous to imagine created beings making either. God can measure creation, but the creation cannot measure God.

Yet human beings think that they can make their gods in some way or other, and Isaiah 40:19 and 20 are a polemic against the whole idea. They focus on the fashioning of Canaanite idols. Unlike many of those of Egypt and elsewhere in Mesopotamia, the idols of Palestine were quite small, usually four to 10 inches tall. They could either be carved from wood,[7] molded in clay (not mentioned here), or cast in metal. This passage focuses on the latter.

The ancient idol maker would use the lost wax method of casting.

After shaping a figure in wax, the craftsman would coat it with clay. Firing it would melt the wax out and harden the now hollow mold. Next the idol manufacturer would pour molten bronze through an opening in the bottom of the feet, leaving a tang, or extension, that could serve as a means of fastening the object to its wooden base. When the metal cooled, the artisan would break the clay mold. Finally, the idol maker would hammer gold or silver leaf onto its surface. Archaeologists have excavated numerous examples of such little idols, some still bearing traces of their gold or silver overlay. And they were supposed to represent deities able to create or maintain a whole world!

Finite people manufacturing their own gods? Ridiculous, Scripture declares. The true God is infinite! From His perspective human beings are like grasshoppers (verse 22). He makes both the universe they live in and controls the history of these ephemeral creatures (verses 22-24). God's "foundations" (verse 21) "shape the fabric of nations and societies as surely as they do the heavens and the stars."[8] Not only is the Lord the Ruler of rulers, but no rival deity exists to challenge or hinder Him.

Again God asks, "To whom then will you compare me,
    or who is my equal? says the Holy One" (verse 25).

Human beings need to learn their finiteness. Look up at the stars, God declares through Isaiah. He created them and controls them (in contrast to the astrologers of Mesopotamia—and of today—who see the stars as controlling humanity). Modern astronomy reveals the vastness and complexity of the visible universe. Our sense of our finiteness should be infinitely greater than that of the people of biblical times, because, seeing the immensity of Creation, we know that God is far beyond what even His prophets could sense. Truly, nothing can be compared with Him!

God's people were struggling to understand how God worked in His world—especially its history. In fact, they wondered if He was involved at all. Had not Assyria and other pagan nations almost destroyed the Davidic kingdom? Was not Jerusalem in constant peril? Did not the threat of exile hang over their head? Yet He claimed to be their God. If so, He should be defending them.

Their Lord knew their questions, and He comforts them and their doubts.

"Why do you say, O Jacob,
    and speak O Israel,
'My way is hidden from the Lord,
    and my right is disregarded by my God'?" (verse 27).

God's people thought that He paid no attention to them, that He was not fulfilling what they saw as His obligations. They knew what the Lord should be doing to save them—but He appeared to do nothing at all. Could He be as oblivious to humanity and its problems, as were many of the pagan gods? Would He ever do anything to help them? But the only answer He could give them was the same one that He presented to the patriarch Job: He was the Creator, and His ways of doing things were, by His very nature, often beyond human understanding (verse 28; cf. Job 38-41). Furthermore, "He does not faint or grow weary" (Isa. 40:28). The ancient Near Eastern gods could become tired and forgetful. They could even die. But the God of Israel and Jacob was the unfailing source of all strength.

Sadly, God's people had not yet grasped all this despite the centuries He had taught and led them (verse 28). God longed to comfort them. But He could do that only as they grasped a sense of who He really was: the Creator of all that is, including the human history that they found themselves trapped in. They needed to learn to "wait" upon their God, to let Him work out things in His time and way.

The Hebrew word here can mean either "wait" or "hope." In this passage "the ideas overlap: 'waiting hope' or 'hopeful waiting.' Israel's impatience and insistence on prompt action from God could become her undoing. An attitude which can wait for the God of the ages and his plan will gain *strength* to *rise* above the moment, *not tire* and *not faint,* but go on and on. The figure of the eagle's wings is apt. The soaring eagle is born aloft not by his powerful wings, but by the wind's currents lifting his rigid pinions. Those *waiting* are those prepared to be lifted up and carried aloft by the spirit of God in his time and his way."[9]

The chiastic structure of verses 10-31 ends the way it began: God is power beyond our comprehension, but He is like a shepherd with His flock; He cares for and strengthens the weak. His people do not understand the working out of His promises any more than the sheep comprehend how the shepherd tends them, but the Lord gives fainting Israel and Jacob strength as long as they remain in His flock.

It is a lesson that God's people still need to learn today. The Lord does not always work in the ways we expect or would like. Often He does things that make no sense to us. The ancients made idols of wood, stone, metal, or clay. We moderns can turn our philosophies, theologies, prophetic charts, or other entities into today's idols. Then we trust in them as did the pagans in their carvings and castings. But it is still idolatry, because we put our faith in something other than God.

God's modern followers are still waiting for Him to establish His eternal kingdom on earth. Why hasn't He come yet? The apparent delay puzzles us. Our faith may wither. The world continues on, and we perish like the grass. But He is still God—He is still the Creator of both the earth and its events. And that is our ultimate guarantee—that He will indeed fulfill His promises. Like Israel and Jacob of old, His creatorship must be the source of our comfort.

God is the ruler of the nations. And in chapter 41 He summons the nations to ponder what that means.

------

[1] J. A. Motyer, *Isaiah: An Introduction and Commentary*, p. 242.

[2] *Ibid.*, pp. 243, 244.

[3] J. H. Walton, V. H. Matthews, and M. W. Chavalas, *The IVP Bible Background Commentary: Old Testament*, p. 625.

[4] Motyer, p. 244.

[5] Walton, Matthews, and Chavalas, p. 626.

[6] See John D. W. Watts, *Isaiah 34-66,* Word Biblical Commentary (Waco, Tex.: Word Books, 1987), vol. 25, pp. 88, 89.

[7] Interestingly, the idol maker here selects a wood that will not rot (Is. 40:20). A god carved out of perishable wood stands in stark contrast to an eternal Creator.

[8] John D. W. Watts, *Isaiah 34-66,* p. 92.

[9] *Ibid.*, pp. 95, 96.

CHAPTER 9

God's Servants

Isaiah 40-66 consists of prophecies of comfort, salvation, and the future glory that God plans for not only the remnant of Israel and Judah but the whole world. The chapters of the second half of the book fall into three obvious sections: 1. God's announcement of deliverance through the future leader of the Medo-Persian Empire, Cyrus (Isa. 40-48). 2. God's depiction of the sufferings of the Lord's "servant" (Isa. 49-57). 3. God's promise of a restored world for both His people and all the nations of the earth (Isa. 58-66). The first two divisions end with the refrain, "There is no peace for the wicked" (Isa. 48:22; 57:21). The third concludes with the wicked extinct (Isa. 66:24).

In previous chapters of this book we have glanced at God's promises of comfort. Now we will look primarily at two agents whom God employs to accomplish His promises.

Allusions to Cyrus first appear in chapter 41. Then the servant who is described as "you, Israel, my servant, Jacob, whom I have chosen" (Isa. 41:8; cf. 44:1-8), the servant who will be a light to the nations (Isa. 42), and the restorer of Israel (Isa. 49). We will examine them in that order. (In chapter 10 we will explore the Suffering Servant of Isaiah 50, 52, and 53.)

All these promises are prophetic. But the fulfillment of any prophecy does not just happen. It is another of God's creative acts. God works behind the scenes, prompting, preventing, adjusting events to make the prophecy come true. When those He calls to do His bidding do not respond, He seeks others. If Satan attempts to thwart a divine plan, God overrules or finds a way around the diabolical roadblock. We marvel at how the Creator can bring matter or life into existence. But how much greater a demonstration of His unfathomable power when He brings His plans to fruition despite the continuing resistance of evil.

Cyrus, My Servant

Most Bible readers see the references to Cyrus as a striking example of God's power to foresee the future. But the book of Isaiah actually presents the Medo-Persian ruler as an illustration of His creative power. In Scripture it is the creative power of the God of Israel that identifies Him as the only true God.

Isaiah 40-45 consists of an extended poem that offers comfort and assurance that God is both real and able to help His people. The Lord will be their redeemer and restorer. The prophet contrasts the God of Israel with the gods of the other nations. He calls the latter nothing more than idols. But Yahweh is real.

One of the key arguments that Isaiah used to demonstrate that God can actually fulfill His promises to Israel is that He knows the future. In Isaiah 41:21-24 God challenges the false gods to prove themselves real. "Set forth your case, says the Lord; bring your proofs, says the King of Jacob. Let them bring forth, and tell us what is to happen. Tell us the former things, what they are, so that we may consider them, and that we may know their outcome; or declare to us the things to come. Tell us what is to come hereafter, that we may know that you are gods."

In Isaiah 44:6, 7, the Lord declares, "I am the first and I am the last; besides me there is no god. Who is like me? Let them proclaim it, let them declare and set it forth before me. Who has announced from of old the things to come? Let them [the false gods, or idols] tell us what is yet to be."

Interestingly, the ancients did not always imagine their gods as having the ability to predict future events. "The future was in the hands of Fate, an impersonal force that controlled the destiny of things. Enki, the god of wisdom, wore a sorcerer's hat, showing that he attempted to control and predict fate, much like a human sorcerer. Fate was written on tablets, and those who controlled the tablets controlled the destiny of the universe. If they were in the wrong hands, there was chaos in the world. . . . At any rate it was not in the god's nature to predict the future, but rather it was a concept they desired to control."[1]

But the true God can foretell what will happen in the future. It is not in the hands of blind fate. Isaiah does not discuss this ability in isolation, however. The prophet presents God's knowledge of the future in the context of that even greater aspect of divine power—His ability to create. These passages appear as part of God's role as Creator.

In Isaiah 40:12-14 God asks, "Who has measured the waters in the hollow of his hand and marked off the heavens with a span, enclosed the dust of the earth in a measure, and weighed the mountains in scales and the hills in a balance? Who has directed the spirit of the Lord, or as his counselor has instructed him? Whom did he consult for his enlightenment, and who taught him the path of justice? Who taught him knowledge and showed him the way of understanding?" The passage echoes what God said to Job out of the whirlwind when He sought to impress upon the patriarch His creative power (Job 38-41).

Isaiah 40:18-20 dismisses idols as nothing more than human-made objects. (The prophet will return to this theme in Isaiah 44:9-20.) But God has existed from the beginning, and He not only created the physical universe, including the earth, but also controls events on our world (Isa. 40:22-24). Things can happen only if God permits them. "To whom then will you compare me, or who is my equal? says the Holy One" (verse 25). The Lord answers His own question by pointing to His creative power. "Lift up your eyes on high and see: Who created these?" (verse 26). "The Lord is the everlasting God, the Creator of the ends of the earth" (verse 28). The true God—the one and only God—is eternal and the Creator of all that is, including human history.

God begins His introduction of Cyrus in Isaiah 41:2 by asking, "Who has roused a victor from the east, summoned him to his service?" It is God's doing. Cyrus began his rise to power in 558 or 559 B.C. when he inherited the throne of his father, Cambyses I, and became king of Persia. Around 556 B.C. the Babylonian king Nabonidus had a dream that prompted him to discard the treaty his country had maintained with the Medes for more than a century and establish a new one with Cyrus.

The vassal kings allied with Media had become frustrated with their overlords. Taking advantage of the discontent, Cyrus rebelled against the Median Empire (strangely enough, governed by his own grandfather, Astyages) and conquered its capital, Ecbatana, in 550 B.C. He thus gained control of an empire comprising what is now modern Iran and extending as far as Armenia. Within another four years he had defeated the Anatolian kingdoms of Lydia and Ionia. Then in 539 B.C. he seized Babylon, putting all of the ancient Near East except Egypt under his rule. Ancient documents depict him as a skilled diplomat able to deal sensitively with the various religions and ethnic groups of his empire. He would set in motion the policies that would allow the exiles from Judah to return to Jerusalem and rebuild the Temple.

In verse 25 the Lord declares, "I stirred up one from the north, and he has come, from the rising of the sun he was summoned by name." God "declared it from the beginning, so that we might know, and beforehand, so that we might say, 'He is right'" (verse 26).

Throughout the passages leading to the mention of Cyrus by name, God keeps returning to the theme of His creatorship. "Thus says God, the Lord, who created the heavens and stretched them out, who spread out the earth and what comes from it, who gives breath to people upon it, and spirit to those who walk in it" (Isa. 42:5).

The Lord promises what He will do for His people Israel. Idols cannot redeem or restore. They cannot create—in fact, as Isaiah has already stressed, they need human beings to bring them into existence (Isa. 40:18-20; 44:9-20). But the God of Israel can create. "It is he who sits above the circle of the earth, . . . who stretches out the heavens like a curtain, and spreads them like a tent to live in; who brings princes to naught, and makes the rulers of the earth as nothing" (Isa. 40:22, 23). Here God links His creative powers with His ability to control political and other events, a point He will develop still further. "The Lord is the everlasting God," He continues, "the Creator of the ends of the earth" (verse 28).

God creates not only the heavens, but also the events that transpire under them. None of this is a new concept in the book of Isaiah. Earlier God had declared concerning the future of Assyria, "As I have designed, so shall it be; and as I have planned, so shall it come to pass" (Isa. 14:24). "For the Lord of hosts has planned, and who will annul it? His hand is stretched out, and who will turn it back?" (verse 27). Prophetic history is as much a divine creative act as the stretching out of the heavens. Just as He brought the world into being, in the same way He makes human history. "I work, and who can hinder it?" (Isa. 43:13). Through His creative power He not only blocks false predictions (Isa. 44:24, 45) but "confirms the word of his servant, and fulfills the prediction of his messengers" (verse 26). And this includes Cyrus, who "is my shepherd, and he shall carry out all my purpose" (verse 28).

Everything Cyrus does he accomplishes only through God's creative activity. The Lord grasps the Persian leader's hand and gives him the power to conquer other nations (Isa. 45:1). The Creator goes ahead of Cyrus to overcome obstacles so that the human leader brings to pass what God wants him to do for His people (verses 2-4). Israel's God arms Cyrus (verse 5) and sets in motion forces that will enable the Persian to fulfill the divine plan. And how can Yahweh do this? Because He is the only God, the Creator who establishes light and darkness and everything else (verses 6, 7). He will arouse Cyrus "in righteousness, and . . . will make all his paths straight" (verse 13), because He is the one "who created the heavens (he is God!), who formed the earth and made it (he established it; he did not create it a chaos, he formed it to be inhabited!): I am the Lord, and there is no other" (verse 18).

History Is Not Passive

But that does not mean that divinely promised events will be automatic or easy. God does not passively watch a history that unfolds all by itself. We belong to a world of creatures that He has granted and endowed with free will. Unfortunately, they have used that freedom to rebel against Him. Satan attempted to usurp God's throne in heaven, and the Creator had to expel the being who had become the devil and chief tempter (Rev. 12:7-9). Then Satan deceived the human race into joining his rebellion, and he, the other fallen angels, and sinful human beings now fight God's plan to redeem humanity and restore the earth. They can resist divine leading. The Lord does not coerce any being. He never rules through arbitrary force—only through love. And He wants every being to accept His leading only through their free will.

In the Garden of Eden the first human couple had to make a choice of whether or not they would obey God (Gen. 3). Even after they ate the forbidden fruit God permitted the human race a large measure of freedom despite their fallen condition. Each individual had to decide whether they would accept or reject Him. They had to choose whether they would participate in or hinder His divine working in human life.

We see this fact illustrated throughout biblical history. When Joshua led the tribes of Israel in their renewal of the covenant with God in the Promised Land, he pleaded for them to rededicate themselves to their Redeemer (Joshua 24:14). Then he added, "Now if you are unwilling to serve the Lord, choose this day whom you will serve, whether the gods your ancestors served in the region beyond the [Euphrates] River or the gods of the Amorites in whose land you are living; but as for me and my household, we will serve the Lord" (verse 15).

Centuries later Elijah demanded of Israel: "How long will you go limping with two different opinions? If the Lord is God, follow him; but if Baal, then follow him" (1 Kings 18:21).

Each human being must make a personal decision. God stands at the door of each life and quietly knocks, but each individual must personally open it and let Him in (Rev. 3:20).

The Lord includes human participation in the outworking of His plans on this same principle. We can choose to serve Him in particular ways—or resist and refuse. Some of the decisions we might make are neither good nor bad. For example, we might select this job instead of that one, take one course of professional training instead of another, or choose to focus on exercising certain spiritual gifts out of a number we might possess.

Other decisions might involve a rejection of God's leading and His plans for our lives. We could refuse to serve Him at all. In that case, God could call another person for the role we should have had, and that individual might fulfill it in a different way than we might have done. God will adapt His plans accordingly to fit the new human situation.

The principle of God working within the constraints of human freedom even touches prophecy. Much biblical prophecy is conditional in nature. Through the prophet Jeremiah God explicitly stated that "at one moment I may declare concerning a nation or a kingdom, that I will pluck up and break down and destroy it, but if that nation, concerning which I have spoken, turns from its evil, I will change my mind about the disaster that I intended to bring on it. And at another moment I may declare concerning a nation or kingdom that I will build and plant it, but if it does evil in my sight, not listening to my voice, then I will change my mind about the good that I had intended to do to it" (Jer. 18:7-10).

The book of Jonah offers a classic example of conditional prophecy in operation. God declared unequivocally through the Israelite prophet that He would destroy the Assyrian capital of Nineveh (Jonah 1:1, 2; 3:1-5). Yet when its inhabitants repented (Jonah 3:5-9) God changed His mind and spared the city (verse 10).

Ezekiel 18:21-24 applies the same principle on the personal level. As we shall see in the book of Isaiah, God could not fulfill many points of prophecy in the way He desired, because Israel and others refused to meet the conditions necessary to bring them to pass.[2]

God is constantly adjusting and setting up new strategies to fulfill His divine promises and plans. He is prepared to deal with any eventuality. Nothing can catch Him off guard. When rebellion or indifference blocks one channel of His working, He opens up another. Similarly He may block or thwart the results of someone's wrong choices. First Samuel 19:18-24 tells how king Saul sent soldiers three times to capture David and bring him back for execution. On each occasion the Holy Spirit interfered, and the soldiers were unable to complete their mission. Finally, in desperation Saul went after David himself, and he found himself caught up in a prophetic "frenzy." God demonstrated to Saul His power, hoping to get the man's attention. Sadly, the king rejected God's leading and resumed his attacks on David's life. However God deals with human response, His goals remain the same.

As God works within the framework of the freedom He has given all creation, He meets each new situation with an appropriate response. Someone may fail to fulfill God's intention, or Satan and the forces of evil may manage to wreck a specific divine scenario. The devil may sow dissension among God's people or pervert governments or other human agencies to fight or persecute God's servants. But God is not thwarted. He has new contingencies, new strategies. Others will respond to His leading when His first choice refuses to do His bidding.

Struggling With the Prince of Persia

Sometimes God will turn immediately to an alternative approach to His goals. Other times He will work mightily to complete His first scenario despite great opposition from His created beings. We see the latter at work especially in God's use of Cyrus as His human agent. In Daniel 10 an angel tells the prophet how for 21 days the "prince of . . . Persia" opposed the heavenly being sent to work out God's plan (Dan. 10:13). Michael, "one of the chief princes," had to come to the aid of the angel. God was encountering fierce resistance, probably from both human and supernatural beings. An omnipotent God could have instantly overwhelmed any creaturely opposition. But He chose not to. Instead, He decided to work within human events, perhaps allowing them to do His bidding from their own motivations, inclinations, and desires. He wants each human decision to be made on the basis of free will. God seeks to convince, to guide, to lead whenever possible.

The God of Israel had made a breakthrough in His plan for Cyrus. The angel could safely come to Daniel and tell him about it. But the opposition was not over yet. Before he left Daniel, the angel announced to the prophet, "Now I must return to fight against the prince of Persia, and when I am through with him, the prince of Greece will come" (verse 20). Michael would have to continue to "contend" with those who struggled to block the prophecy (verse 21).

As we have seen repeatedly, God's working in human affairs and history is just as much a manifestation of His creative power as bringing matter and life into existence. Prophecy does not fulfill itself. The Creator brings it to pass. He is constantly striving to make it happen. Many Christians have considered God's greatest power to be the ability to see the future. But which is the greater power—to foresee something that will take place no matter what, or to make it happen in a universe in which free will can oppose and even frustrate divine intervention?

Other Christians have become so fascinated with the predictions of prophecy that they forget the One who brings them to pass. Prophecy is not the account of the inevitable—it is the story of a mighty God working out His awesome intentions. Something is predestined only because God guarantees through His personal intervention that it will actually take place.

As one author put it, "In the annals of human history the growth of nations, the rise and fall of empires, appear as dependent on the will and prowess of man. The shaping of events seems, to a large degree, to be determined by his power, ambition, or caprice. But in the Word of God the curtain is drawn aside, and we behold, behind, above, and through all the play and counterplay of human interests and power and passions, the agencies of the all-merciful One, silently, patiently working out the counsels of His own will."[3]

For the prophet Isaiah, our assurance about the future rests ultimately not on divine foreknowledge but on God's divine creatorship and the power it manifests. Prophecy comes true because He is the true God. Idols can do nothing, but the God of Israel is the Creator. Thus the prophet could predict Cyrus and have complete confidence that God would bring His servant into existence.

"Remember this and consider,
 recall it to mind, you transgressors,
 remember the former things of old;
for I am God, and there is no other;
 I am God, and there is no one like me,
declaring the end from the beginning
 and from ancient times things not yet done,
saying, 'My purpose shall stand,
 and I will fulfill my intention,'
calling a bird of prey from the east,
 the man for my purpose from a far country.
I have spoken, *and I will bring it to pass;*
 I have planned, *and I will do it*" (Isa. 46:8–11).

God creates His intended future. He does not sit idly waiting for it. We must never let prediction overshadow the God who makes that future.

My Servant Israel

The book of Isaiah employs the image of a servant in a number of senses, but they seem to progress from a human and earthly aspect to something more. Isaiah speaks of the servant both collectively and as an individual (Isa. 41:8-10; 42:1-9, 18-22; 43:10; 44:1-5, 21-28; 45:4; 48:20-22).

The first servant passage begins with a legal hearing, a kind of cosmic trial. God summons the nations along the coast of Palestine (Isa. 41:1) to show that He alone is God because only He can predict the future. A new power is emerging on the international horizon. Can it be resisted? The coastal nations seek encouragement from each other and from idols (verses 5-7). But the people of Israel are also concerned. Has the Lord abandoned them? What should they do?

God speaks to Israel, declaring that He has chosen them as His servant (verse 8) since the time of Abraham (verses 8, 9). He has not cast them off (verse 9). Rather, "Do not fear, for I am with you, do not be afraid, for I am your God" (verse 10). The Lord will strengthen and help them (verses 10, 13). Their enemies will vanish in disgrace (verses 11, 12). Although they might feel as powerless and worthless as a worm or insect (verse 14), God will make of them a "threshing sledge" (verse 15).

The sledge was a device consisting of a heavy platform of wood embedded with stone or iron teeth that a donkey or other draft animal pulled over the harvested barley or wheat to separate the grain from the chaff before the winnowing. Israel would become God's agent to prepare the earth for the final harvest (verses 15, 16). God's servant here is a human institution divinely commissioned and empowered to act as His agent on earth. In Isaiah 44:21 God reminds His people that they are His servant and that He will not forget them. After all, He has redeemed them, sweeping away their transgressions like a cloud (verse 22). But they must accept that role by their own choice.

Light to the Gentiles

The imagery of the servant begins to shift in Isaiah 42. Throughout this section God has discussed His political agent, Cyrus, who will set in motion the events that will lead to the restoration of Israel and the transformation of the world. But the Lord needs still another agent—a spiritual one. Through this second agent God will bring justice to an unjust world, because He has empowered him with His Spirit (Isa. 42:1). Many commentators stress the gentleness of a servant who will not break a damaged reed or extinguish a lamp wick about to go out because its fuel is gone (verse 3). But the implication is also that this servant can fix a damaged reed or replenish the supply of oil.

Furthermore, he has the strength to finish his difficult task (verse 4). He will be "a light to the nations" (verse 6). This servant will be God's agent of salvation for the whole world. He will redeem not only those taken into exile but also the Gentiles. God's servant will be able to accomplish for the latter what their idols—their gods—cannot. His mission echoes that of Abraham and his "seed" (Gen. 12:3; 18:18; 22:18; 26:4). The context of this description of the servant is that of God's people redeemed and restored to the Promised Land. But the language has more than the human streaming through it. Even in Isaiah 42 the task requires divine power (verses 1, 6). It calls for the supernatural. Jesus, whom the New Testament calls the New Israel.[4] Jesus had every right to apply this passage from Isaiah to Himself (Luke 4:16-21).

The Lord guarantees that He will not only raise up such a servant but also enable that servant to accomplish the mission given. He points to the fact that He is Creator—creator of the universe and sustainer of life (verse 5). The wonder of such a promise elicits a hymn of praise (verses 10-20).

Restorer of Israel

The servant passage in Isaiah 49 shifts the perspective from a collective people to a single individual. He is still called Israel (Isa. 49:3), but his role includes leading Israel as a people back to God (verses 5, 6). Therefore the divinely chosen agent cannot be the people as a whole. "This Servant Israel ([Isa. 49:] 3) is, first, distinct from the nation Israel, for it is his task to bring the people back: the nation cannot be its own saviour from sin. Secondly, he is the true and only Israel, for he is going to do what Israel was always meant to do (cf. [Isa.] 2:2-4)—gather from the whole world."[5] God called this servant even before his birth (verse 1), but he feels that his mission has been a failure (verse 4). As in Isaiah 42, the servant is to be a light and source of salvation to the whole earth (verse 6). "This task runs beyond what any prophet or any mere human could fulfill."[6]

Although verse 7 describes the servant as "the slave of rulers," the Lord regards Him as worthy of great honor. Paul in Philippians 2:5-11 reflects this imagery of a servant/slave receiving homage and honor. Though nations may abhor the servant, rulers still honor and submit to Him. Isaiah 52:13ff. will develop this theme even further. As the Lord's servant, He will lead God's people home in a New Exodus from all the places of their exile (Isa. 49:10-12). Isaiah 49:8-10 echoes Isaiah 42:6, 7.

This servant whom rulers prostrate themselves before must be the Davidic King described in the first half of the book. He is a righteous king.

Again Isaiah uses imagery that even the Gentiles could understand. "In Assyrian literature the just reign of a king is characterized by prosperity, diligent worship, rejoicing, freeing prisoners, healing of sickness, anointing with oil, and providing food and clothing for the needy. Similar elements are projected for Yahweh's restoration of his people and become part of the messianic profile."[7] As the prophet sees all that God will do through His servant, we can understand why he proclaims:

"Sing for joy, O heavens, and exult O earth;
break forth, O mountains, into singing!
For the Lord has comforted his people,
and will have compassion on his suffering ones" (Isa. 49:13).

The image of the servant is growing larger than any human being. The earthly is ripping away to reveal glimpses of the divine. But the Suffering Servant passages of Isaiah 50, 52, and 53 will open even more fully to our view His cosmic nature.

---

[1] J. H. Walton, V. H. Matthews, and M. W. Chavalas, *The IVP Bible Background Commentary: Old Testament,* p. 628.

[2] For a thoughtful though older discussion of the concept of conditional prophecy, especially in the case of Israel, see "The Role of Israel in Old Testament Prophecy," *The Seventh-day Adventist Bible Commentary* (Washington, D.C.: Review and Herald Pub. Assn., 1977), vol. 4, pp. 25-38.

[3] Ellen G. White, *Education* (Mountain View, Calif.: Pacific Press Pub. Assn., 1903), p. 173.

[4] See Jon Paulien, *The Deep Things of God,* chap. 8.

[5] J. A. Motyer, *Isaiah: An Introduction and Commentary,* p. 310, 311.

[6] *Ibid.,* p. 311.

[7] Walton, Matthews, and Chavalas, p. 632.

CHAPTER 10

The Mysterious Servant

God has been assuring His people that He will restore them. He tells them of a glorious future that He plans for them (Isa. 49:8-26). But they still feel abandoned. Their situation does not appear to have improved. The Lord recognizes and comforts their discouragement. First, though, He asks, Have I really rejected you? Where's the evidence? Show it to Me, He requests. "Where is your mother's bill of divorce with which I put her away? Or which of my creditors is it to whom I have sold you?" (Isa. 50:1). The oracle presents the former nations of Judah and Israel as a mother and the exiles as her children. People in the ancient world unable to pay off a loan or other debt could be sold into slavery. Desperate families might have to sell some of their members into bondage just to survive. Did God do that to His people?

The Lord has not rejected them, He declares. It is the other way around. In reality He is the offended party in this cosmic marital relationship. His people have turned away from Him. Israel is in exile because of their own sins (verse 1). They have not responded to His call (verse 2). But as for their future, "Is my hand shortened, that it cannot redeem? Or have I no power to deliver?" (verse 2). Israel may have been sold into slavery, but God has the money to buy them back. Surely a deity who can do dramatic things to the earth, its living beings, and the sky above (verses 2, 3) has the power to save His people.

The Vindicated Servant

Suddenly a new voice enters the oracle. Someone begins to speak in first person. God has given this individual the ability to sustain the "weary" (verse 4). It is the same word Isaiah 40:28, 29 uses when the passage declares that God will give "power to the faint." This agent accepts his mission (verse 5) even though it inflicts abuse upon him (verse 6). People of the ancient world (and their descendants in the Middle East today) were particularly sensitive to insults or anything that would bring shame and dishonor. But God's agent ignores such concerns. The knowledge that the Lord is with him enables him to face anything that comes his way (verse 7). He will let nothing overwhelm him. In verse 8 the prophet uses legal terminology. The servant stands on trial. But he is confident that all charges against him will be proved false. "Who will contend with me? . . . Who are my adversaries? Let them confront me" (verse 8). God's agent has complete trust in Him.

Clearly the servant is more than Israel. God's people are not innocent, as is the servant. In fact, they have been sold into slavery because of their sins. "When seen in the larger context of the narrative movement within chapters 40-55, there is a clear transfer from Israel, the servant nation, to Israel, the suffering individual who now embodies the nation's true mission."[1]

Some modern commentators have attempted to identify certain historical persons as the servant described here.[2] Such individuals might have been among God's human agents on earth helping to work out divine plans, but the language of the servant passages keeps going beyond any specific human beings. The servant is far more than all of them combined. As we constantly see, the servant surpasses the merely human. Like the figure of the king of Babylon earlier, the servant here points beyond itself to a cosmic level. The book of Isaiah keeps leading the reader to the universal war of which human situations are merely a surface manifestation. When human kings go to war, it reflects the ultimate conflict between supernatural rulers.

The servant is confident that the cosmic court hearing will not prove him guilty because the Lord, the absolutely just and honest judge, makes it clear to all in the supernatural trial that His servant is innocent of every charge against him (verse 9). No accusation can stand against the truth of who he is.

The oracle again shifts perspective. It is no longer the servant speaking—he is now spoken about. Scripture now asks:

> "Who among you fears the Lord
>> and obeys the voice of his servant,[3]
>> who walks in darkness and has no light
> yet trusts in the name of the Lord
>> and relies upon his God?" (verse 10).

Childs suggests that here "a challenge is extended to anyone who rightly fears the Lord, and thus identifies with the message of the servant, to trust in God even though it involves walking on a path of darkness, just like the servant."[4] Unlike Israel as a whole, the servant is willing to trust God and His power even though he does not know all the details of how God is working out His plan to redeem His people. Yet in his faith he accomplishes great things. The servant will be a light to all nations, including Israel. But those who attempt to make their own light will face only disappointment and bitter punishment from God (verse 11).

The Suffering Servant

After more glorious promises of restoration for Israel (Isa. 51:1-52:12) the prophet again returns to the theme of God's special servant (Isa. 52:13-53:12). Here Isaiah will focus on the servant's suffering and what it means for both Israel and all the nations.

Isaiah 52:13 declares that the servant will prosper and be exalted. But then verses 14 and 15 do an abrupt shift. His appearance is now marred "beyond human semblance" (verse 14). Something has happened that astounds the nations (verse 15). In addition, a special group begins to understand the significance of the servant's experience. The words "for that which had not been told them they shall see, and that which they had not heard they shall contemplate" (verse 15) echoes the passage "You have heard; now see all this. . . . From this time forward I make you hear new things, hidden things that you have not known" of Isaiah 48:6 (cf. verses 7, 8). In Isaiah 53:1-12 that group confesses their growing understanding of the meaning of what the servant has gone through.[5]

The speakers of Isaiah 53:1 have had divinely revealed to them that the servant is the "arm of the Lord." Yet he is truly human (verses 2, 3). Because he grew up "before" the Lord he is distinct from Him. And he is a specific person, not collective Israel or a faithful remnant as many commentators argue.[6] "The language cannot be rendered metaphorically as the nation without straining the plain sense of the text in a tortuous fashion."[7]

The servant was shunned and misunderstood by those who had no sense of who he was.

"He had no form or majesty that we should look at him,
    nothing in his appearance that we should desire him.
He was despised and rejected by others;
    a man of suffering [or "man of sorrows"] and acquainted
        with infirmity,
and as one from whom others hide their faces[8]
he was despised, and we held him of no account" (verses 2, 3).

John later declared this prediction of rejection as fulfilled in the experience of Jesus (John 1:10, 11).

To onlookers the servant seemed to be undergoing punishment by God. But what he endured was not for what he had done, but for the sins of others.

> "Surely he has born our infirmities
>> and carried our diseases;[9]
> yet we account him stricken,
>> struck down by God, and afflicted" (verse 4).

Paradoxically, the servant suffers, but he is an exalted being. In fact, Isaiah 52:1 speaks of him in metaphors that reflect the transcendence of God Himself.[10] How can that be? It would have made little sense to most of the prophet's hearers. As we see in the book of Job, ancient Israel equated prosperity with God's approval, poverty and suffering with divine displeasure. Isaiah has to explain why the servant suffered yet could be exalted.

> "He was wounded for our transgressions,
>> crushed for our iniquities" (verse 5).

Scripture uses the word "crushed" to describe agony ending in death, as in Lamentations 3:34. The punishment God's agent received made "us whole," and through the bruises he endured "we are healed" (Isa. 53: 5). Because "we like sheep" have wandered away from the divine Shepherd "the Lord has laid on him the iniquity of us all" (verse 6). Yes, the servant suffered, and yes, God afflicted him—but it was so the Lord could lay "our" sins on him. He suffered for "our" benefit. And in a very real sense Isaiah sees what the servant did as what the Lord Himself also did. The "man of sorrows" has taken upon himself the sorrows of all humanity, freeing us from their grief and burden.

Although the servant was oppressed and afflicted, he did not protest or defend himself. He remained silent like a lamb being taken to slaughter and a sheep being sheared (verse 7). His fate represented a total perversion of justice, and he was "cut off" from the living (verse 8). The Hebrew for "cut off" has the implication of "hacked off," as in 1 Kings 3:25. To add to his sufferings he experienced the pain of a total lack of understanding of what he was going through. Only through revelation would humanity gain insight into his mission.

The servant did not oppose God's people, nor was his heart filled with deceit. Still, his enemies buried him with the wicked, thus declaring their opinion of him (Isa. 53:9). Yet all that happened to him was

God's will, because his life was an offering for sin (verse 10). Leviticus 4:1-6:7 describes the guilt offering that the servant's death reflects. Motyer observes that the offering "could well be called the 'satisfaction offering.' It is used here not so much to affirm that the Servant bore and discharged the guiltiness of our sin, but that what he did is exactly equivalent to what needed to be done." [11] While we cannot understand all the implications of the atonement, the suffering servant met every requirement to save humanity.

God's servant perishes and is buried. But he is alive in the end—"he shall see his offspring, and shall prolong his days" (Isa. 53:10). Because what the servant did was according to divine will, it would have meaning and significance. "The righteous one, my servant, shall make many righteous, and he shall bear their iniquities" (verse 11). He not only would transform the status of those of God's people who would accept his sacrifice, but would cleanse them of their sin. They would no longer be the wicked that the Lord confronts in Isaiah 1.

The servant's death was not the end of his existence. He had won a wondrous victory and would reap its rewards.

"Therefore I will allot him a portion with the great [the many],
and he shall divide the spoil with the strong" (Isa. 53:12).

Suffering has resulted in a great triumph for the servant. Verse 12 sees his cosmic success and exaltation as resting on four facts.

1. "He poured out himself to death"—he voluntarily suffered to the point of death.
2. "He . . . was numbered with the transgressors"—he identified with those who needed salvation.
3. "He bore the sin of many"—he was an effective substitute for lost humanity. His life and death had the power to accomplish what needed to be done to save sinful human beings.
4. "He . . . made intercession"—he interceded and mediated for those he desired to save.

Thus "the dead ([Isa. 53:] 9) is alive ([verse] 10), the condemned ([verse] 8) is righteous ([verse] 11), the helpless ([verse] 7) is the victor ([verse] 12)." [12]

The Substitute King

While the full depths of what the servant would do would not be revealed until the cross, the Gentiles who read Isaiah during the prophet's lifetime could catch a sense of what the experience of the suffering servant meant. Once more God spoke in imagery that would communicate beyond His people.

Assyria had a custom that would give them some insight into the meaning of the suffering servant. As mentioned before, astrology was rampant in Mesopotamia. People believed that humanity was controlled by the decrees of fate. But the stars and astronomical bodies would give clues to what might happen. When the casting of a horoscope, or an astronomical phenomenon such as an eclipse, indicated that the life of the king might be threatened, his counselors would resort to a practice called the rite of the substitute king. The Assyrians believed that evil could be transferred from one person to another. They would replace the king with someone else during the period when the danger would supposedly fall. The idea was that the threat would strike the substitute instead of the real ruler.

The chosen individual would be someone regarded as of no importance. The person might even be mentally or physically impaired. He would exercise the formalities of kingship perhaps for as long as 100 days. During that period the real king would remain in isolation and would undergo various purification rites. Eventually, though, the substitute king would be put to death and given a state funeral along with exorcism rituals. His execution was considered a canceling of the threat against the actual ruler.[13]

The suffering servant did not save one individual only, but all who would accept its results. He was far more than a social reject—he was the "arm of the Lord." But the Assyrian custom at least would help the Gentiles (and those of Israel who knew of the practice) to recognize God's desire to save others.

As with the previous servant passages, there follows an invitation to participate in the salvation accomplished through his sacrifice. Isaiah 54:1-55:13 speaks first to the "barren women" of Zion, then to all who want to attend the Messianic feast. Isaiah 54 and 55 correspond to Isaiah 40:1-42:17, which depicts the message of comfort expanding into worldwide blessing. Christ would later apply the theme of the Messianic banquet (as He did the suffering servant imagery) to Himself (Matt. 22:1-14; Luke 14:15-24).

---

[1] B. S. Childs, *Isaiah*, p. 395.

[2] For example, see the work of John D. W. Watts, *Isaiah 34-66*, pp. 199-204.

[3] Motyer points out that "Lord" and "servant" are parallel to each other and suggests that "the way to reverence the Lord is to obey the servant" (J. A. Motyer, *Isaiah: An Introduction and Commentary*, p. 319).

[4] Childs, p. 396.

[5] "The connection between the new [literary] unit and the preceding divine speech is skillfully made with a chiastic device. The metaphor of seeing (Isa. 52:15b and Isa. 53:1b) brackets that of hearing (Isa. 52:15b and Isa. 53:1a) and confirms the continuity between the group of Israel in Isaiah 52:15b and the confessing voice of Isa. 53:1ff." (Childs, p. 413).

[6] For typical Jewish interpretations, see I. W. Slotki, *Isaiah*, p. 260, and The Jewish Bible, pp. 890-892.

[7] Childs, p. 414.

[8] The phrase can also be translated as "one who hid his face from us." The Messiah did not hide His face in the sense of rejecting humanity, but of cloaking who He was during His life as a human being on earth (Phil. 2:5-8).

[9] The biblical world considered disease as divine punishment.

[10] Gerald T. Shepherd, "Isaiah," *The HarperCollins Bible Commentary,* ed. James L. Mays (San Francisco: HarperSanFrancisco, 2000), p. 527.

[11] Motyer, p. 338.

[12] *Ibid.*

- 13 Walton, Matthews, and Chavalas, pp. 633, 634.

CHAPTER 11

Divine Delights

God has assured Israel that He will redeem and restore them. But that promise and its glorious benefits are not limited just to Israel. The Lord wants all nations to be His people. Too often believers have read Isaiah 55 as speaking only to them. But God brings Israel back for a specific mission—they are to represent Him to the nations of the world. A careful reading of this divine mission reveals its inclusiveness.

Palestine had limited sources of water. Aside from the Jordan, it had almost no streams that flowed year-round. The people depended on a few springs, such as the Gihon in Jerusalem, and water stored in cisterns during the short rainy season. But God urges "everyone who thirsts, come to the waters" (Isa. 55:1). And in a world in which most were poor, barely eking out survival from one harvest to another, the offer to those without money to "come, buy and eat" must have seemed beyond imagination.

They can "delight" themselves in rich food. The prophet will expand that image of "delight" in the next few chapters. God, however, has more than literal food in mind. "Why do you spend your money for that which is not bread, and your labor for that which does not satisfy?" (verse 2). The Lord wants to establish an "everlasting covenant" beyond that which He had made with David (verse 3; see 2 Sam. 7:8-16; 23:5; 1 Kings 8:23-26; Ps. 89:27-37). The first Davidic covenant had been with just David himself, but now the expanded covenant applies to God's people as a whole.

David had been a witness for God (Isa. 55:3, 4), but restored Israel will be an even greater witness. "See, you shall call nations that you do not know, and nations that do not know you shall run to you, because of the Lord your God, the Holy One of Israel, for he has glorified you" (verse 5). The language echoes David's self-description in Psalm 18:43, 44: "People whom I had not known served me. . . . Foreigners came cringing to me." Now the nations would come, not out of fear, but from joy. In succeeding chapters the prophet will continue this theme of foreigners joining God's people.

Such a promise is not automatic. It must be responded to before it can be received. God's people must seek the Lord while He continues to hold out His offer (Isa. 55:6). The wicked must return to the Lord and accept His astounding mercy and pardon (verse 7). Christians, familiar with the New Testament teaching of love forever demonstrated at the cross, do not sense how radical God's offer must have seemed to the people of the Old Testament (and to those in other cultures even today). Human justice demands that evil must receive its recompense if life is to be fair. How can we forgive someone who has raped and murdered our child? Can we pardon those who committed the Holocaust or terrorist acts? Even if they asked for our forgiveness, would we be able to give it to them? Justice seems to demand that they suffer in some way. What human court would rescind punishment simply because the guilty asked for forgiveness?

But God can.

> "For my thoughts are not your thoughts,
> nor are your ways my ways, says the Lord.
> For as the heavens are higher than the earth,
> so are my ways higher than your ways
> and my thoughts than your thoughts" (verses 8, 9).

The gods of the ancient world were little more than superpowerful human beings. They exhibited the same character traits and behavior as humanity and were subject to the same flaws, such as hatred, cruelty, envy, jealousy, and unfaithfulness. The God of Israel, however, was different. He was "the Lord, the Lord, a God merciful and gracious, slow to anger, and abounding in steadfast love and faithfulness, keeping steadfast love for the thousandth generation, forgiving iniquity and transgression and sin" (Ex. 34:6, 7).

As we have seen repeatedly, God is Creator not just of the world but of history. Just as the rain and snow do not return to the heavens until they have brought forth life and nourishment in a parched land, so God's word will not come back to Him until it has accomplished what He intends. (Interestingly, the New Testament often describes Jesus, God's agent of salvation, as the Word. See, for example, John 1:1 and Revelation 19:13.) But if God's people do return to Him, they will return to their home in great joy (Isa. 55:12). Not only will they be brought back to the land, but the land will be restored as the cypress replaces the thorn and the myrtle the brier:

"It shall be to the Lord for a memorial,
    for an everlasting sign that shall not be cut off" (verse 13).

The Sabbath—Sign of God's People

The latter half of Isaiah discusses the Sabbath twice (Isa. 56:2, 4; 58:13). In both cases it is presented as an integral part of the life of the true follower of God. In many ways Scripture treats the concepts of the Sabbath and God's people as two sides of a single coin, the coin of Creation. Where you find one aspect you will frequently find the other.

Genesis associates the Sabbath with the creation of the first human beings, the beginning of all peoples (Gen. 1:1-2:3). After the Exodus, God had to instill in the former Hebrew slaves a sense of identity as a distinct people. First, as they wandered across the desolate wilderness they struggled with the temptation to retreat to the familiar and comforting foods of the Nile Valley. To assure them that He would care for them God began the weekly miracle of the gift of manna (Ex. 16:13-36). Manna fell six days of the week, including a double portion on the sixth day, and none on the Sabbath. Their obedience to the manna cycle and their rest on the Sabbath became a test of their acceptance of God as their Lord and themselves as His people.

Next God led the Hebrews to Mount Sinai, where He declared them "a priestly kingdom and a holy nation" (Ex. 19:6). From Sinai God proclaimed the Ten Commandments. He prefaced the Decalogue with the statement that they now stood on the plain before Sinai only because He had delivered them from their bondage. "I am the Lord your God, who brought you out of the land of Egypt, out of the house of slavery" (Ex. 20:2). They were a distinct and free nation only because of His doing.

But they were not to be an exclusive people. God made provision to include others, as we see in the special laws for the sojourner, or resident alien. Israelite law granted resident aliens Sabbath rest (Ex. 20:10; 23:12; Deut. 5:14); the right to a fair trial (Deut. 1:16); permission to flee to the cities of refuge (Num. 35:15; Joshua 20:9); and participation in Israelite religious celebrations, including the Feasts of Booths and Weeks (Deut. 16:10, 11, 13, 14), the Day of Atonement (Lev. 16:29, 30), and the Passover (Ex. 12:48, 49; Num. 9:14).

Like the Israelites, sojourners had to refrain from consuming blood (Lev. 17:10), could not blaspheme God's name (Lev. 24:16), and needed to observe the regulations involving the ashes of the red heifer sacrifice (Num. 19:2-10) and other sacrifices (Lev. 17:8, 9; 22:18-20; Num. 15:14-

16). They could obtain atonement for sin (Num. 15:26-31). In addition, they had to observe sexual and moral purity (Lev. 18:26).

To provide for their economic support, they could glean from the crops (Lev. 19:10; 23:22) and receive the triennial tithe (Deut. 26:12) and the produce of the land during the sabbatical year (Lev. 25:6).

The rights and duties of the sojourners reflect those of Israel itself. They were even part of the assembly when God renewed the covenant with His people after they entered the Promised Land (Joshua 8:30-35). But they received such rights only if they identified with the covenant community (Ex. 12:43-49). Such laws provided a way to incorporate those who wanted to become part of God's people. The Lord had said that Abraham was to be a blessing to the nations, and his descendants were to witness to the world until the God of Abraham, Isaac, and Jacob was the God of all the nations.

The fourth commandment reminded them that God had created the first human beings (Ex. 20:11). It was a theme that appeared frequently during the wilderness sojourn as God sought to form them as His people (Ex. 31:16, 17). The Sabbath was a symbol of their new peoplehood.

The Sabbath is prominent not only in the biblical narrative of the formation of God's people, but it also surfaces whenever His people face the threat of destruction, assimilation, or dispersion. For example, 2 Kings 11 tells how Athaliah, the queen mother of the Judahite king Ahaziah, and daughter of Ahab and Jezebel of Israel, usurped control of Judah after her son's death. She attempted to destroy all the royal family. But Ahaziah's sister, Jehosheba, managed to save Ahaziah's son Joash and hide him in the Temple precincts for six years. In the seventh year Jehoiada, the high priest, staged a coup to remove Athaliah from power and put Joash on the throne. The coup took place on the Sabbath (2 Kings 11:5-9). After Athaliah had been executed, Jehoiada made "a covenant between the Lord and the king and people, that they should be the Lord's people" (verse 17).

The changing of the guard on Sabbath allowed Jehoiada to assemble all of the Temple guards at one time without attracting immediate suspicion, and the reference to Sabbath could be dismissed as just that. But the Bible rarely goes into great detail about anything. Its style is characteristically terse and incorporates only what the author considers vital. Thus when Scripture does mention what at first might seem to be a minor point, we must pay special attention to it. It is there for a reason. The Bible includes something only to make a point. The author of 2 Kings could have described the coup without referring to what day it was. But by mentioning the Sabbath along

106

with the making of a covenant between God and the people, the author is directing the reader's attention to the Sinai experience. The people who have almost been destroyed by the activities of Athaliah are now reconstituted and brought back into relationship with God.

Amos 8 reports that materialism and economic abuse had become rampant in the northern kingdom. In their desire for gain they could not wait until the Sabbath had ended to resume their business activities. Scripture contrasts Israel's covenant with God and with each other symbolized by the Sabbath with the self-destructive practices that were tearing God's people apart.

Just before the destruction of Jerusalem by the forces of Babylon, the prophet Jeremiah emphasized the Sabbath (Jer. 17:19-27). Judah faced extermination as a nation and even as a people. If they would but observe the Sabbath, Jerusalem would be inhabited forever (verses 24-26). But they refused to listen to the prophet and "stiffened their necks and would not hear or receive instruction" (verse 23).

References to the Sabbath also appear during the Exile and afterward. Before we look at what Isaiah has to say about it, we will continue to examine its relationship to the identity and stability of God's people in the rest of Scripture. In Ezekiel God sketches the history of His people before announcing that He will restore Israel, bringing them back from their exile (Eze. 20). Twice He mentions that the Sabbath was a sign or symbol of His relationship to them as a people (Eze. 20:12, 20).

When some of the exiles do return from Babylon, the Sabbath again makes an appearance. As Nehemiah works to restore the identity of religious life in Jerusalem he finds that its inhabitants, in league with the people around, have turned the Sabbath into just another market day (Neh. 13:15- 22). The passage specifically mentions non-Israelites—Tyrians— who were bringing in fish and other merchandise and using the Sabbath as their business day (verse 16).

The context of the incident is the danger of assimilation that threatens the people of Jerusalem. Non-Israelites are moving into the city and even the Temple (verses 1-9). Many of God's people, including one of the sons of the high priest, had non-Israelite wives (verses 23-30). The children of such marriages could not even speak their fathers' language. Nehemiah stressed the Sabbath as a symbol of their identity as God's people and of their allegiance to Him.

In the Old Testament God's representatives stressed the Sabbath as a way of holding the people together and preserving their identity. Many ignored or rejected its observance. But after the experience of exile some swung to the other extreme. They now rigidly observed the Sabbath, by New Testament times transforming it into a barrier that isolated Israel from the other nations. Throughout the book of Isaiah God had promised that the other nations would join Israel. By Jesus' time some religious factions had made the Sabbath into a symbol of exclusiveness. It had become a burden. Jesus in His Sabbath miracles sought to remove all trappings that would discourage others from joining God's people. As in Isaiah, God's goal is to make all the nations His people.

Sabbath in Isaiah

Both Sabbath passages in Isaiah appear in two major contexts. The first is that of worship, the acknowledgment of humanity's relationship to the Creator of the universe and their response to His power, nature, and accomplishments. The second is that of restoration. The Sabbath passages also occur in a larger section of the book that displays four identifiable parts. The entire section contrasts a worldwide "Sabbath people" (Isa. 56:1-8) with Israel's actual condition (Isa. 56:9-57:21). Isaiah 58:1-4 presents the theme of life centered on the Sabbath as God's ideal for His people, but then the prophet confesses that the people have yet to reach that goal (Isa. 59:1-15). The book of Isaiah does not dwell in idealistic fantasy. While it depicts God's glorious goals, it recognizes that a transformation must yet take place in His people. But the God who can create the universe (of which the Sabbath is a symbol) can re-create His people (also symbolized by the Sabbath).

The major emphases of the Old Testament prophets were justice and ethical relationships. The prophets were more interested in how we should treat others than what would happen in the future. They spoke more of economics and social relationships than last-day events. Isaiah presents the Lord's message that summons His people to "maintain justice, and do what is right, for soon my salvation will come, and my deliverance be revealed" (Isa. 56:1).

A true commitment to God involves doing right to others. Those who do right will receive God's blessing, especially those who honor the Sabbath (verse 2). The Sabbath was the special symbol of the covenant between God and His people (Ex. 31:13-17; Jer. 17:21-27; Eze. 20:20, 21). To honor the Sabbath was to honor God and acknowledge who He was and what He was doing for and with His people. Sabbath worship was a demonstration of one's commitment to Him.

Motyer comments that "some scholars, referring to Nehemiah 10:31 and 13:15, would see this emphasis on the Sabbath as evidence of a post-exilic date. But Isaiah 1:13 and Amos 8:5 show how punctilious was Sabbath observance in the pre-exile. Ezekiel 20:12; 22:8, 26, condemn profaning the Sabbath as a pre-exilic sin, and Jeremiah 17:19-27 makes Sabbath observance a test of obedience to the Lord. Isaiah makes the same point. Acceptance of the Sabbath involves the reorganization of the whole of life in order to accommodate the principle of one day set apart; it is also the Lord's invitation to his covenant people (Ex. 31:16) to enter into his rest (Ex. 23:12; 31:17). There could be no plainer testimony to belonging to the Lord's separated people."[1]

The prophet gives two specific illustrations of how the Sabbath can work in the life of a believer: the foreigner and the eunuch. Throughout history those born outside a group find it difficult to be accepted by that group. And the eunuch was a second-class citizen in Israel. He could neither be part of the assembly of the Lord (Deut. 23:1), nor preserve his name through any posterity. But God declares, "Do not let the foreigner joined to the Lord say, 'The Lord will surely separate me from his people'; and do not let the eunuch say, 'I am just a dry tree'" (Isa. 56:3).

The eunuch who observes the Sabbath and does what pleases God will have a monument better than offspring. The Lord will take both the eunuch and the foreigner to His holy mountain "and make them joyful in my house of prayer" (verse 7). God will accept their offerings and sacrifices, unlike some of those presented by people born in the covenant community (Isa. 1:11-15), and they can speak directly with Him. (Did Philip the evangelist especially direct the Ethiopian eunuch to this passage?).

Many in Israel, like their pagan neighbors, had viewed the Temple as a place solely for cultic and ritualistic ceremonies. But God had always wanted it to be a place of prayer for all peoples. And at the restoration it would be. Not only would God bring back the exiles; He would at last fulfil His intent for His people: it would be an ever-growing community that would eventually encompass all humanity. "Thus says the Lord God, who gathers the outcasts of Israel, I will gather others to them besides those already gathered" (Isa. 56:8).

The second discussion of the Sabbath appears in Isaiah 58, a section dealing with false and true worship. Such worship is a much broader concept than what is usually done in temple or church. It involves the entirety of the way we live.

God commands Isaiah to announce Israel's rebellion (Isa. 58:1). Yet their apostasy is a subtle one. They actually believe that they are quite dedicated to Him. Daily they seek Him "as if they were a nation that practiced righteousness and did not forsake the ordinance of their God" (verse 2). God's people think that they "delight" to know His ways and draw near to Him. But they are only deluding themselves. The Lord selects an example of their meaningless religious life: fasting. Fasting was a practice not common in the ancient Near East except among Israelites. Although they may be deceiving themselves about their religious condition, they still sense that something is wrong. God is not paying attention as they expect He should. "Why do we fast, but you do not see? Why humble ourselves, but you do not notice?" (verse 3).

The Lord is blunt in His response. "Look, you serve your own interest on your fast day, and oppress all your workers" (verse 3). Their religion does not extend beyond the Temple to their daily lives. They perform religious ritual, then defraud others. (Economic exploitation is not new.) True religion is not ritual and ceremony, but how we treat others (cf. James 1:27). Many of God's people carefully fast, then leave the place of worship and abuse others. "Such fasting as you do today will not make your voice heard on high" (Isa. 58:4).

After describing their fasting rituals, God explains what true fasting is (verses 6, 7, 9, 10). It is not abasing the body, but caring for others. Biblical religion does not focus so much on the personal as on social relationships. The kind of fast the Lord longs for from His people is for them to eliminate injustice, free the oppressed, feed the hungry, make the homeless part of their family, and suppress gossip and slander. (In Hammurabi's law code the pointing of the finger, as in verse 9, was part of a formal accusation.) Nor will they shirk their responsibility for their own kin (verse 7). If they will do all this, then God will hear their petitions (verses 9-12).

The Lord finds Israel's fasts unacceptable because His people are doing it for their own self-interest. The same principle stands behind His command about the Sabbath. They cannot call the Sabbath a delight if they are going their own way, seeking their own advantage, and pursuing their own affairs (verse 13). But if they observe the Sabbath in a way that truly does bring them the right kind of delight, they will also delight in the Lord, and He will be able to honor and bless them in the manner He longs to (verse 14). God condemns a religion that assumes it has a relationship with God while trying to avoid a relationship with others.[2]

"The Sabbath is not observed as a means of manipulating God or to realize any ulterior motive. Rather, one celebrates the day by focusing one's attention on the majestic words of God in creation (Ex. 20:11) and on salvation (Deut. 5:15). The observance of the Sabbath by God's faithful is only pleasing as an act of worship that takes delight in God. As such it is fully congruent with the stipulation for the obedient response of feeding the hungry and caring for the poor."[3]

The Sabbath both transforms God's people and provides the conditions they need to expand until they include all peoples and nations.

Since the Sabbath was an integral part of the book of Isaiah, the use of imagery or allusions in the book of Revelation from passages surrounding those chapters in Isaiah that mention the Sabbath would remind the New Testament reader of the larger literary context without explicitly mentioning it. By implication they would sense that the Sabbath would have a role to play in the final cosmic conflict between good and evil, just as it had in the Old Testament scenario. The book of Revelation thus indicates that the Sabbath will once again become a fundamental symbol of the identity of the establishment of God's people.

––––––––––

[1] J. A. Motyer, *Isaiah: An Introduction and Commentary*, pp. 350, 351. Cf. B. S. Childs' comment that "while it is true that in the postexilic period the emphasis on Sabbath observance greatly increased in importance as the means of expressing obedience to God under the restraints of postexilic life without political autonomy . . . , these commands serve as a concrete expression of the selfsame will of God on which the original Mosaic covenant was based and are not a descent into narrow legalism, as has frequently been charged by Christian antinomians" (B. S. Childs, *Isaiah,* p. 458).

[2] Motyer, p. 360.

[3] Childs, p. 481.

CHAPTER 12

Only God Can Rescue

Righteousness in the Old Testament world was a highly practical and concrete thing. It was not a philosophical or spiritual abstraction, but the way one lived. When the prophets called God's people to righteousness, they spoke about how Israel should live as a society—how they should treat others. Righteousness involved matters of economics and social justice as well as ethics and ritual purity. In fact, in a sense one could call such righteousness in the Old Testament a social gospel. Sin was defrauding and abusing others and violating culturally approved relationships.

We have already seen how God declares that He rejects worship and fasting from those who take advantage of others (Isa. 58). In Judah social conflict raged on every hand. The wealthy had the upper hand through their use of power and social advantage. In Isaiah 59 the Lord declares that sin is really injustice, and that He must punish those who mistreat their fellow human beings. But before He deals with their condition, He reminds them of His own: "See, the Lord's hand is not too short to save, nor his ear too dull to hear" (Isa. 59:1).

His declaration is in response to the question that throughout Isaiah is uppermost in His people's minds: "Why hasn't our salvation come yet?" Is He unable to answer their prayers and thus not deserving of worship? God has the power to redeem His people. There can be no question about that. As He has repeatedly reminded Israel, He is the Creator. But He cannot respond to them now because of their condition. The Lord tells them, "Your iniquities have been barriers between you and your God, and your sins have hidden his face from you so that he does not hear" (verse 2). The noise of their crimes drowns out their pleas.

God begins to catalog their iniquities (echoing those of chapter 58). First, they have blood on their hands (verse 3). One commentator suggests that the blood represents economic pressure on the poor,[1] though verse 7 does seem more clearly to indicate actual murder. But even then, putting others in impossible financial situations in which they cannot support themselves will kill them just as surely as knives or poison. The Lord's people utter lies and slander (verse 3) and pervert justice and the legal system, particularly by bringing unfair lawsuits against the defenseless (verse 4). The last part of verse 5 portrays the people as pregnant with evil and iniquity. Instead of giving birth to life, they create death.

In verses 5 and 6 they symbolically hatch poisonous serpents and weave clothing out of insubstantial spiderwebs, which cannot cover their nakedness. Society is breaking down, no person can trust another, and it is dangerous to travel because of banditry (verse 7). There may be both literal and metaphoric truth in this statement. Crime committed on the trade routes would affect everyone. A decline in trade would create economic depression and more poverty, intensifying the pressure on the disadvantaged. Those who distort justice for their own gain are making crooked paths that lead to suffering and oppression. Society is an intricately interwoven fabric. If it frays or is turned to the advantage of a privileged few, the vast majority suffer.

Not only does society lack justice, but it has no peace (verse 8). In Hebrew thought, peace *(shalom)* was not just an absence of violence; it was a positive condition. *Shalom* "as a harmonious state of the soul and mind encourages the development of the faculties and powers."[2] It has connotations of wholeness, health, and personal welfare. All this, the oracle declares, has vanished from Israelite society. While the prophet does not specify to whom the oracle is addressed, it would be those with power and wealth whom he would consider responsible for the problem.[3]

The oracle declares of those responsible for creating such conditions that the roads or paths they have made are crooked (verse 8), an allusion in reverse to the book's theme of making the way straight for the Lord (Isa. 40:3; cf. 42:16; 45:2).

Verses 9-14 of Isaiah 59 present a "community lamentation," a literary form that appears frequently in the book of Psalms. The unnamed "us" acknowledges that God's people lack justice and righteousness. They are in darkness and need light (verse 9) just as much as the Gentiles. God's people, who are clearly the implied speaker, need the "light to the nations"—God's servant—as much as the rest of the world. It is the only thing that will solve any of humanity's problems. God's community admits their transgressions and iniquities, their lack of justice and righteousness (verses 12-14). In fact, Israelite society has become so warped that it seeks to destroy anyone who does turn away from evil (verse 15).

The Divine Warrior

The situation is beyond any human remedy. It requires a divine solution, as the Lord clearly recognizes (verses 15, 16). "Appalled" by the fact that there was no one to intervene, He, through "his own arm," brings about the victory (verse 16). "Arm" directs the reader back to the statements about the "arm" of the Lord in Isaiah 52:10 and 53:1. Instead of proclaiming judgment against His people, (in Isa. 59:9-15 they admit their guilt), He sets out to save them (verses 16-20).

The Lord girds Himself for battle.

"He put on righteousness like a breastplate,
  and a helmet of salvation on his head;[4]
he put on garments of vengeance for clothing,
  and wrapped himself in fury as a mantle" (verse 17).

God has become the divine warrior. As we saw earlier, the ancients believed that their gods fought for them. If they won, it was because their deity defeated that of their opponents. But here the God of Israel really does wage warfare for His people.

God wears divine armor. But what does the imagery mean? Two of the things He puts on particularly puzzle the contemporary Western mind: the "garments of vengeance" and "fury" "as a mantle" (verse 17). "The word 'vengeance' presents the modern reader with a wrong idea. *Naqam* means 'vindication' rendered without fear or favor (cf. [Isa.] 35:4), for God's action is both destruction and salvation in one (cf. Luke 18:7). 'Fury' is that concentration of purpose which we call 'zeal.' Its meaning is well expressed at John 2:17 when Jesus' disciples quoted Ps. 69:9 in reference to Jesus' cleansing of the temple: 'Zeal for thy house has consumed me.'"[5]

The Lord is able to redeem and transform His rebellious people, to bring them justice, righteousness, and truth. His power bursts into the world as He comes "like a pent-up stream that the wind of the Lord drives on" (Isa. 59:19). He is a rushing wind or spirit (the Hebrew word means both), able to create a new history for Zion just as the Spirit brought into being a new world at Creation (verse 19). He will redeem those who turn away from transgression.

As God had stepped into history to deliver Israel from Egyptian slavery and made a covenant with them at Sinai, so He once again intervenes and renews His covenant (verse 21). And He does something else. Long

114

ago Moses had longed, "Would that all the Lord's people were prophets, and that the Lord would put his spirit in them" (Num. 11:29). Now God would make such a thing actually come to pass. During the time of His restoration of Israel He will fill His people with His Spirit. The inspired words He gives them they in turn teach to each new generation.

Light Has Begun to Dawn

Isaiah 59:9 speaks about a need for light. A herald of salvation now announces that light (Isa. 60:1-3). Many commentators consider him to be the servant that has appeared earlier. The light has begun to dawn (verse 1) as chapters 60 and 61 return to the theme of the future blessedness of God's people. God has come to them, and His revealed glory shines through them. As Jesus said, God's people must and will be lamps to illuminate the world (Matt. 5:14-16). The light starts in Zion and spreads to the rest of the world, progressively banishing the darkness that envelopes it. As the glory of the Lord radiates from Jerusalem, it attracts the rest of humanity, drawing it to Him. In descriptions that parallel Isaiah 2, chapter 60 tells how the people of the earth flock to Zion. "Nations shall come to your light, and kings to the brightness of your dawn" (Isa. 60:3).

The oracle commands Israel to look up and see the exiles being brought back to them (verses 4-9). They are carried in their nurses' arms (verse 4), an ancient image depicting the most personal care possible.[6] The wealth of the nations, particularly represented by items used in the Temple services, shall come to Jerusalem (verses 5-7). The oracle cites several examples of tribes or peoples then regarded as rich. The nations give not from coercion but because of their awe and appreciation of the God who has redeemed and transformed Israel. The kings, impressed by what they have seen, then lead their own people to the God of Israel. The world will do all this because of what God has done for Zion (verse 9). The foreigners mentioned in verse 10 are not servants or slaves but full members of God's community committed to His service. (Those nations, however, who reject God will eventually perish [verse 12].)

So many pilgrims are coming and going in Jerusalem that the city gates are never closed. Visitors are always welcome. And there is no need to shut the gates anyway. The ancients locked their city gates because of the threat of enemy attack or the incursions of criminals. But that danger has passed. Jerusalem is truly a city of "peace," the *shalom* part of its name. Zion is whole and fulfilled. The book of Revelation picks up this imagery to show the peace and safety of the New Jerusalem (Rev. 21:25).

In Isaiah 60:14 the descendants of nations that once oppressed Israel now bow before God's people. They do so "in order to enter the privileges and joys of Zion. Only a triumph of grace could achieve this, for it is not Zion that produces this ready submissiveness but the recognition that *the Lord* is in his *City* in all his reality as *the Holy One of Israel.*"[7]

God will take His people, once forsaken and hated, and make them majestic and an eternal joy (verse 15). The oracle reverts to the imagery of verse 4 and has them wet-nursed by nations and kings (verse 16). No longer will they wonder whether God is their Savior and Redeemer—they will know without question (verse 16). The Lord transforms Zion materially and socially (verse 17) and spiritually (verse 18).

The people of the ancient Near East considered the sun and moon to be gods and worshiped them. The Babylonians especially honored Sin, their moon god. The Creation account in Genesis dismissed them as just created objects instead of deities by not even mentioning them by name since that would be to the speak the names of pagan gods (Gen. 1:14-18). Now the oracle of Isaiah even ignores them as light givers. The people of Zion will not need sunlight or moonlight, for the Lord will be their source of radiance (verses 19, 20). He is their light as well as that to the nations. Revelation 21:23 employs this imagery.[8]

The oracle of the suffering servant promises that He shall have offspring (Isa. 53:10). Now the servant has them—righteous and planted[9] in the land forever (Isa. 60:21). And it will happen, because the Lord Himself will accomplish it (verse 22).

The Spirit of the Lord

Isaiah 61, building upon concepts in Isaiah 42:1 and Isaiah 49:1-5, has a first-person voice declaring, "The spirit of the Lord God is upon me" (Isa. 61:1; cf. Isa. 11:2; 42:1). The Spirit compels the speaker to do great and wonderful things as the Spirit did in Genesis 1. He receives the Spirit "because the Lord has anointed me" (Isa. 61:1). The term *Messiah* comes from the Hebrew for "anointed." The Lord has sent His anointed one— His Messiah—"to bring good news ['gospel'] to the oppressed, to bind up the brokenhearted, to proclaim liberty to the captives, and release to the prisoners" (verse 1). The speaker says that he will "bandage" the wounded and free those imprisoned by circumstances. The image of release would resonate even with Gentiles. During the first year or two of their reigns, kings of the ancient Near East often freed people from debtor's prison as an act of grace. Again, as with previous servant passages, commentators have identified this speaker with Israel as a people or even the prophet himself, but the verses offer still another example of language that strains to reveal something beyond and greater than humanity.

Yes, a human being can release prisoners and comfort the afflicted and the other wonderful things in verses 1-4, but verses 5-7 echo the promises of restoration that the Lord Himself has made earlier in Isaiah. The servant here is identifying with the God of Israel. He can speak for God because He is the "arm" of God—He is God. Thus, as we have mentioned previously, Jesus, the Son of God, could take this and its parallel passages in Isaiah as the outline and summary of His mission on earth (Luke 4:16-21). The Servant not only frees and comforts, but transforms the world so that nothing will again imprison, wound, or cause anyone to mourn. As a result of His work God's people become oaks of righteousness that He has planted (verse 3).

Israel as a whole supported those of its number who served as priests. But during the restoration the nations will contribute their wealth so that all of Israel may be priests for the whole world (verse 6). Later Jesus would commission the Christian church as a priesthood for all humanity (1 Peter 2:5; Rev. 1:6).

As with the servant passage of Isaiah 49, God confirms His covenant with His people (Isa. 61:7-9). He makes that covenant on the basis of His divine nature—He is a God of justice who now has a people that reflect that justice. Verses 9-11 reflect a commitment to God's mission. Some commentators see this passage as the servant's acceptance, others as that of God's people. The imagery could apply to both, but Isaiah elsewhere uses it to refer to Israel (Isa. 49:18), and the book of Revelation employs it to describe God's people as His bride (Rev. 21:2). But the commitment is all the Lord's doing.

> "For as the earth brings forth its shoots
>> and as a garden causes what is sown in it to spring up,
> so the Lord God will cause righteousness and praise
>> to spring up before all the nations" (Isa. 61:11).

---

[1] George A. F. Knight, *The New Israel: A Commentary on the Book of Isaiah 56-66* (Grand Rapids: Wm. B. Eerdmans Pub. Co., 1985), p. 34.

[2] W. E. Vine, Merrill F. Unger, and William White, Jr., *Vine's Complete Expository Dictionary of Old and New Testament Words* (Nashville: Thomas Nelson Publishers, 1996), p. 174.

[3] John L. McKenzie, *Second Isaiah: Introduction, Translation, and Notes* (Garden City, N.Y.: Doubleday, 1968), p. 172.

[4] In Ephesians 6:10-17 Paul applies this imagery to the individual Christian.

[5] Knight, p. 37.

[6] The Egyptians would often show in painting and sculpture their kings being suckled by goddesses. They had divine wet nurses.

[7] J. A. Motyer, *Isaiah: An Introduction and Commentary,* p. 374.

[8] Some focus on the "scientific" aspects of the verse and miss the real point. Knight comments that we should keep in mind that the oracle is speaking metaphorically "about the grace of a God whose loving purpose can never be adequately described in human terms" (p. 48).

[9] The first shoot is the promised and righteous king, the shoot of Jesse. The true righteous Israel, He makes other righteous shoots that form a new and redeemed Israel.

CHAPTER 13

The Future Restoration

Throughout the book of Isaiah we have seen God continually returning to Israel's implied question of when and how will He finally redeem them. Isaiah 62:1-63:6 portrays that salvation as drawing closer. The nations will watch as Zion ceases to be desolate and receives a symbolic new name—Hephzibah, "My Delight Is in Her" (Isa. 62:4). The Lord will vanquish Zion's enemies, represented by one in particular: Edom (Isa. 63:1-6). Edom had taken advantage of Judah's weakness by raiding and seizing her territory. In Isaiah 63:7-64:12 God's people pray to Him, recounting His dealings with them (Isa. 63:7-14) and reminding Him that He is their Father and Redeemer (Isa. 63:16; 64:8). All but overwhelmed by the fear that He has abandoned them (Isa. 63:19), they beg Him to intervene (Isa. 64:1, 2), and acknowledge their guilt (verse 6).

Finally, in chapters 65 and 66 He gives His fullest response to the question of redemption and restoration. He explains that He can save only those who have truly committed themselves to Him. All others He will have to punish, and in Isaiah 65 He lists examples of those "who provoke me to my face continually" (Isa. 65:3). Besides the worship of nonexistent gods, some of the practices seek the aid of the dead (verse 4) and other forces to manipulate events—to make a history of humanity's own choosing. In verse 11 He condemns those "who set a table for Fortune and fill cups of mixed wine for Destiny." Throughout the book of Isaiah God has emphasized how He is the Creator not only of the world but of history, too. To worship deities of fate[1] would be to blatantly reject God's control of events.

The Lord will redeem and restore Israel both by intervening in history and by bringing to pass a glorious new creation. It is the new creation that we will look at now. But it is the outcome of a specific divine history that God seeks to establish—a scenario of last-day events.

Isaiah's Understanding of the Last Days

The book of Isaiah presents many details of how God hoped to restore Israel and then expand His people until they included all the nations of the earth. We have seen some of these promises in previous chapters, especially chapter 12. Other aspects focus on divine judgment. Besides the many warnings of judgment against Israel and Judah scattered through the first half of the book of Isaiah,[2] the prophet also depicts God announcing judgment against the nations of the earth.[3] "The earth shall be utterly laid waste and utterly despoiled" (Isa. 24:3). "For the Lord is enraged against all the nations . . . ; he has doomed them, has given them over for slaughter. . . . All the host of heaven shall rot away, and the skies roll up like a scroll" (Isa. 34:2-4).

God would spread death and destruction across the earth, but it would not be total. Many of the nations would survive and (as we have already seen) would, under God's leading, help His scattered remnant return to Palestine. The theme of the exiles restored to Judah and Israel is woven throughout the book.

After He brought the captives back to the Promised Land, God would transform the land. At one time forest had covered perhaps 60 percent of Palestine. An expanding population had cleared much of it for cropland. Then military invasions had repeatedly devastated the land. Such enemy forces would cut down large numbers of trees to construct siege machines and fortifications. It was also common for marauding armies to chop down orchards and destroy vineyards to weaken the local population by reducing its food resources. The disruption of normal farm activities and the deportation of the peasants allowed the soil of agricultural terraces to erode away or become overgrown with briers and other wild vegetation. The fragile ecology of Palestine unraveled under such assaults. But God would now make Zion's "wilderness like Eden, her desert like the garden of the Lord" (Isa. 51:3).

Then, in their revitalized home, the people of Judah and Israel—now one people—would glorify the Lord (Isa. 49:3) as they witness to and praise His power and the fact that He is the only true God (Isa. 43:10, 21; 44:8). They would be "a light to the nations, that my salvation may reach to the end of the earth" (Isa. 49:6; cf. Isa. 42:6, 7). The Lord would send representatives from His people to other nations (Isa. 66:19; cf. Isa. 42:12). Observing what God was doing with His people, the Gentiles would acknowledge how He blessed His people (Isa. 61:9) and that their God was indeed the only true God (Isa. 45:14). The light of truth would shine from Jerusalem (Isa. 2:3; 60:3). God would call to all humanity, "Turn to me and be saved, all the ends of the earth! For I am God, and there is no other" (Isa. 45:22).

People from all parts of the globe would flock to Palestine (Isa. 14:1; 45:14; 49:12, 18, 22; 56:6, 7; 60:3). The divine blessing showered on Israel would attract the attention of nations that had never previously heard of God's chosen people, and they would come to Jerusalem (Isa. 55:5). The Temple in Jerusalem would be called "a house of prayer for all peoples" (Isa. 56:7). Inspired by what they saw and wanting to participate themselves, the nations would bring their wealth and service to Jerusalem (Isa. 45:14; 60:1-11; 61:5, 6), resources that God's people could use to reach still other nations. Even God's former enemies would worship the Lord and be His people (Isa. 19:18-24). "In days to come Jacob shall take root, Israel shall blossom and put forth shoots, and fill the whole world with fruit" (Isa. 27:6). The whole world would be the Promised Land.

Notice that in the book of Isaiah God transforms the world gradually. It involves no catastrophic global conflict, no colossal battle of Armageddon as portrayed in other Old Testament prophetic writings and especially in the New Testament.[4] The nearest the book comes to a violent struggle are hints in such chapters as Isaiah 6, 8, 13, 17, 60, and 66. Often speaking about great darkness covering the earth, the warnings are directed against God's rebellious people as much as the other nations. In Isaiah 66:15 and 16 God comes in fire. But after the threat eases against God's people, the world changes peacefully. We do not find the clearly enunciated attacks on Jerusalem depicted, for example, in Jeremiah 25, Ezekiel 38, Joel 3, and Zechariah 12. Isaiah does mention, though, that the Lord will destroy Babylon (Isa. 13).

A Glorious New Creation

The final part of the book of Isaiah presents a more fully detailed view of that world God wants to create for His redeemed people. The prophet has made many allusions to a restored people and world, but chapters 65 and 66 present that restoration in two sections that depict God's new handiwork. The first appears in Isaiah 65:17-25.

Verse 17 declares that God is "about to create new heavens and a new earth." Scripture uses the Hebrew word for "creating" with only God as its subject. The early chapters of Genesis have it nine times and Isaiah 40-66 employs it 19 times (Isaiah 45 six times and Isaiah 65:17 and 18 three times).[5] His new creation will have a dramatic impact on the people.

When God said that "the former things shall not be remembered or come to mind" (Isa. 65:17), He was not indicating that the redeemed will undergo some kind of collective amnesia. If He blanked out of their memory everything they had experienced, His people would have learned nothing from their tumultuous history. A humanity that has forgotten what sin does would be just as vulnerable to succumbing to it again as Adam and Eve were. And if God took away freedom of will, it would make a mockery of all that the redeemed had gone through. They would have suffered for nothing. Rather, their "awareness will be of total newness. . . . The new creation will be observed and enjoyed by new, fresh minds."[6] They will not be surrounded by sin-damaged reminders of what once was. Yes, they will have memories of sin's consequences, but they will not be confronted by it at every turn.

The new world will be one of gladness and joy. Words that reflect this appear six times in Isaiah 65:18 and 19. Both humanity and God experience that joy. The saved rejoice in the new creation and their God, and He "delights" in them and in Jerusalem. The new creation will also be a dramatic change from the old world. The old and new creations stand in stark contrast between each other.

The world will no longer have:	But it will have:
Crying, distress	Rejoicing
An infant dying after a few days of life	A child living to be 100
Adults dying prematurely	Age 100 considered an early death
Building homes for someone else to live in	Building homes and getting to live in them
Planting for someone else to seize and eat	Planting vineyards and eating from them
Work for no reward	Life spans like that of a tree
Giving birth to children who face a life of terror	Offspring blessed
Unanswered prayer	God answering before people pray
Unending violence	Nothing that will harm or destroy in God's holy mountain[7]

The prophetic promises use imagery that the people know. They reflect a pastoral world, an extension of the one they already live in. "The new is portrayed wholly in terms of the old, only without the old sorrows;

there is no attempt to describe any other kind of newness."[8] In line with the rest of the scenario presented in the book of Isaiah, the restoration is gradual. Some major changes take place early, as in the transformation of predators (Isa. 65:25). (Dust as food for the serpent is an allusion to Genesis 3:14.) Other things may take time, such as a gradual extension of life. The death of someone at age 100 is compared to that of a dying child (verse 20). The description of the new creation does not say that death is yet abolished. Isaiah 25:7, 8 does predict the destruction of death, but that is apparently yet future.[9] Isaiah as a whole presents a step-by-step evangelization of the earth, which would mean that death could not be eliminated until all humanity had made a clear choice for or against God during Israel's evangelization of the earth. Until then life would be extended as a token of the ultimate restoration.

After a discussion of the kind of worship God desires or rejects, and more promises that He will vindicate Zion and destroy its enemies (Isa. 66:1-17),[10] the Lord returns to His frequent theme of Israel's return from exile, and evangelization of the world (verses 18-21). God will even choose Gentiles to be His priests and Levites (verses 20, 21; cf. Isa. 56:6-8). Then God's people shall be as eternal as the new creation itself. And so shall be the worship of all the redeemed from both Israel and all the nations. "All flesh shall come to worship before me, says the Lord," "from sabbath to sabbath." Throughout eternity the Sabbath will be the symbol of God's people, fully formed people at last (Isa. 66:23).

Sadly, Israel failed to accept God's offer. Much in the book of Isaiah is only "what could have been." God could not progressively transform the world. His people continued in their rebellion. After their return from exile they withdrew into themselves and largely lost their sense of mission to the world. But God did not give up. He did not focus on Israel's failure and His disappointment. Nor was He willing to settle for a lesser fulfillment. God finds another way to accomplish His dreams for humanity, something even greater.

For example, the New Testament declares that when God does come to restore the world at Jesus' second coming He will not just give us progressively longer and longer life. Instead, He will instantly abolish death altogether (1 Cor. 15:54, 55; Rev. 21:4). Although contrary humanity may foil one approach, the Lord comes up with an even more magnificent one. God has unlimited power to create and re-create the flow of history, despite both human and demonic resistance. That power is His proof that He is the one and only true God.

Isaiah's failed scenario, however, provided imagery that other biblical writers would use to describe the new plans God revealed through later prophets. As we have mentioned previously, the book of Revelation (especially the later chapters) contains numerous allusions to, and echoes of, the book of Isaiah. We saw some of them in the introduction.

By New Testament times scriptural authors would often employ a brief biblical text, phrase, or image to represent a larger passage or collection of texts. Such biblical allusions act as a shorthand way of presenting a larger concept that the new prophet would reveal in God's developing plan. The book of Revelation employs images from Isaiah as it presents its view of last-day events. The Lord will fulfill His promises in ways that are both new and yet echo what Scripture has already announced. God is both consistent and ever creative.

The Camp of the Wicked Has Perished

As mentioned previously, the first two sections of the latter half of Isaiah (40-48 and 49-57) end with the refrain "There is no peace for the wicked" (48:22; 57:21). Some of the wicked have accepted God's forgiveness and are no longer evil. Now the book ends as abruptly as it began, with the unrepentant wicked experiencing an ironic kind of peace—they have ceased to exist. God destroys those determined to remain in rebellion against Him. Isaiah 66:24 jars the modern Western reader, but it finishes the pattern and assures us that the restoration is eternal. It echoes the experience of the camp of the Assyrians just outside Jerusalem—"When morning dawned, they were all dead bodies" (Isa. 37:36). Like Assyria, all who attack God's people are flaunting their God and will in the end perish.[11]

Isaiah 66:24 is also the counterpart to the beginning of Isaiah. Chapter 1 proclaimed the wickedness of Judah and especially Jerusalem. At last, rebellion and apostasy have come to an end, and God's people are purified. The wicked are gone forever, and their fate assures the redeemed that justice and righteousness will reign throughout eternity. God's people will never again have anything to fear from evil.

The good news proclaimed by Isaiah that the Lord is the God of the nations is at last fully true, and all the redeemed live in peace and security on a restored earth. Kings will no longer go to war. True, that has not yet happened, but the promise is guaranteed, because the righteous King "Prince of Peace" has come. The Man of Sorrows has set in operation the plan that will bring an end to all sorrows. As both halves of the book of Isaiah declare (Isa. 35:10; 51:11), sorrow will flee from God's people, and they shall return to Him with joy and singing. Jesus is now at work to complete the final stages of salvation. And we can have total trust in Him because He is the all-powerful Creator.

---

[1] J. H. Walton, V. H. Matthews, and M. W. Chavalas, *The IVP Bible Background Commentary: Old Testament,* pp. 640, 641; B. S. Childs, *Isaiah,* pp. 536, 537.

[2] See, for example, Isaiah 1:7, 8, 24, 25; 2:10-21; 3:25, 26; 5:25-30; 8:5-8; 9:19-21; 22:1-8; 28:21-29.

[3] Isaiah presents many oracles against specific nations, especially in chapters 13-21; 23; 47. Chapter 13 employs "day of the Lord" imagery against Babylon. The judgment becomes even broader in chapters 24 and 34.

[4] Paulien discusses the various biblical scenarios for the end-time, ranging from peaceful to violent ones. See his *What the Bible Says About the End-time* (pp. 54-64) for those presented by the later Old Testament prophets, including Isaiah.

[5] John D. W. Watts, *Isaiah 34-66,* p. 353.

[6] J. A. Motyer, *Isaiah: An Introduction and Commentary,* p. 398.

[7] Adapted from Watts, *Isaiah 34-36,* p. 354.

[8] D. Kidner, "Isaiah," p. 669.

[9] Motyer argues (p. 399) that the reference to someone dying at 100 is only metaphor.

[10] Verse 17 with its image of pagan and other false worship echoes the polemic against corrupt worship of chapter 1.

[11] Jewish tradition repeats Isaiah 66:23 after verse 24 so that the book will end on a positive note (*Jewish Study Bible,* p. 916). Margaret Becker sees the reference to those who have "rebelled" against God as an allusion to fallen angels ("Isaiah," p. 541).